LEITH'S
BOOK OF CAKES

LEITH'S
BOOK OF CAKES

Fiona Burrell

Foreword by Caroline Waldegrave

Photographs by Graham Kirk

BLOOMSBURY

For Charles

First published in Great Britain 1995
Bloomsbury Publishing Plc, 2 Soho Square, London W1V 5DE

Copyright ©1995 by Leith's School of Food and Wine Ltd

The moral right of the author has been asserted

A CIP catalogue record for this book is
available from the British Library

ISBN 0 7475 2190 5

10 9 8 7 6 5 4 3 2 1

Typeset by Hewer Text Composition Services, Edinburgh
Printed by Butler and Tanner Ltd, Frome, Somerset

Photographer: Graham Kirk
Stylist: Helen Payne
Home economists: Puff Fairclough and Valeria Sisti
Line drawings by: Kate Simunek

CONTENTS

ACKNOWLEDGEMENTS

This book could not have been written without the help and encouragement of my colleagues, friends and family.

I would like to thank the teachers at Leith's School of Food and Wine who have tested and tasted the recipes with great enthusiasm. I would particularly like to thank Caroline Waldegrave for all her support, and for putting her faith in me.

Caroline Yates deciphered my often illegible handwriting, and typed the recipes that were sometimes written on a bumpy train or with a baby on my knee! She never complained, and I am enormously grateful to her for her help and also for giving me some of her cake recipes to use in the book. I would also like to thank Judy van der Sande and Annie Simmonds for doing extra typing for me at very little notice.

Puff Fairclough cooked the cakes for the photographs, assisted by Valeria Sisti, and put a great deal of time and effort into making sure they were exactly as I wanted them. I am extremely grateful to both of them, and to Graham Kirk who took the photographs.

This book could not have been produced without the editorial expertise of Helen Dore.

I gratefully acknowledge the help of the Dried Fruit Information Service, who provided me not only with information, but also with dried fruit for testing recipes and for using in the photographs.

Lastly, I would like to thank my husband, Charles Stevenson, for his never ending support and his willingness to eat his way through all the cakes, and also my daughter, Evie, for allowing me to finish the book when she was only four weeks old.

FOREWORD

This book is a mixture of recipes that have always been on the curriculum at Leith's School of Food & Wine and others that Fiona has collected in the course of her professional career, including some from friends and family. Fiona has always been the queen of baking at Leith's School: ask her a technical question about the chemical reaction of bicarbonate of soda with yoghurt or about the best way to cope with a curdled cake mixture and she always has the definitive answer ready for you.

Every recipe has been thoroughly tested but we are very conscious of how much baking times can vary depending on ovens, ingredients and equipment. For example, a fan oven will dry any cake. The larger the cake, the drier it will tend to be. Heat is conducted through different materials at different rates, so baking times will vary a little by and large. Even ingredients will affect baking times; for example, stale almonds cook faster than fresh, oily ones.

I do hope that you enjoy baking from this book.

CAROLINE WALDEGRAVE
Principal, Leith's School of Food and Wine

INTRODUCTION

One of my earliest childhood memories is sitting on the kitchen table while my mother mixed a cake. As a special treat I was allowed to scrape out the bowl. That always seemed to be the best part of cake-making. Later on I was allowed to make cakes on my own, and like many other people, I think this was my first venture into cooking. Many children still cut their culinary teeth on cake-making. It can be relatively easy and the results are tempting and delicious.

Nowadays, people tend to make cakes because they enjoy making them, rather than from necessity. Largely gone are the days when tea-time was a daily ritual. At 4.30 p.m. the tea table or tray would be set with scones, cakes and biscuits, all home-made. Nowadays we live life on the run and time is short. Baking cakes is often something done at the weekends or for a special occasion. It is a very satisfying form of cooking: the smell of the cakes baking in the oven is both evocative and welcoming. Most modern kitchens are equipped with machines that remove the hard labour from cake-making. Even the simplest electric hand beater takes the sweat out of the beating and whisking that some cakes demand.

During the writing of this book, I have been given much advice on what people would like to find in a cake book. There are cakes for every occasion. Some are very simple and quick to make, others are more complicated. Some of the cake recipes would be suitable to use as a pudding, which can be useful if you are providing a birthday cake at the end of a meal. I have not included novelty party cakes because they are better covered in other books devoted solely to them. However, there are instructions on how to make, marzipan and ice a rich fruit cake for a celebration.

All the recipes indicate the size of cake tin to be used and this is crucial for successful cakes. If you use a larger tin, the cake will take less time to bake than specified in the recipe, and may turn out dry, while a smaller tin will result in the cake overflowing in the oven. Also remember, however, that every oven varies, so the times given in the recipes can only be approximate: your oven may be slower or faster than the one we used to test the cakes. Fan ovens cook more quickly, even at a lower temperature, and can dry out cakes.

If a cake becomes dark on top during baking, but is not cooked in the middle (see page 26), turn the oven temperature down and cover it with a piece of greaseproof paper.

During the first three-quarters of baking time cakes are quite unstable, so do not be tempted to open the oven door and move the cakes around the oven while they are baking. This can result in a beautiful-looking cake sinking in the middle. Unfortunately, once a cake has sunk nothing will persuade it to rise again. Sinking is more of a problem with sponge cakes; rich fruit cakes are more stable.

Unless specified, the eggs used in the recipe are size 3 and the sugar used is caster sugar. The spoon measurements used are the standard measuring spoons. If you use ordinary spoons the measurement should be gently rounded, not heaped unless specified.

I hope you enjoy not only the making of the cakes in this book, but also, more importantly, the eating of them.

FIONA BURRELL

Conversion Tables

The tables below are approximate, and do not conform in all respects to the conventional conversions, but we have found them convenient for cooking. Use either metric or imperial measurements. But do not mix the two.

Weight

Imperial	Metric	Imperial	Metric
¼oz	7–8g	½oz	15g
¾oz	20g	1oz	30g
2oz	55g	3oz	85g
4oz (¼lb)	110g	5oz	140g
6oz	170g	7oz	200g
8oz (½lb)	225g	9oz	255g
10oz	285g	11oz	310g
12oz (¾lb)	340g	13oz	370g
14oz	400g	15oz	425g
16oz (1lb)	450g	1¼lb	560g
1½lb	675g	2lb	900g
3lb	1.35kg	4lb	1.8kg
5lb	2.3kg	6lb	2.7kg
7lb	3.2kg	8lb	3.6kg
9lb	4.0kg	10lb	4.5kg

Australian cup measures

	Metric	Imperial
1 cup flour	140g	5oz
1 cup sugar (crystal or caster)	225g	8oz
1 cup brown sugar, firmly packed	170g	6oz
1 cup icing sugar, sifted	170g	6oz
1 cup butter	225g	8oz
1 cup honey, golden syrup, treacle	370g	12oz
1 cup fresh breadcrumbs	55g	2oz
1 cup crushed biscuit crumbs	110g	4oz
1 cup mixed fruit or individual fruit, such as sultanas	170g	6oz
1 cup nuts, chopped	110g	4oz
1 cup coconut, desiccated	85g	3oz

Approximate American/European conversions

	USA	Metric	Imperial
Flour	1 cup	140g	5oz
Caster and granulated sugar	1 cup	225g	8oz
Caster and granulated sugar	2 level tablespoons	30g	1oz
Brown sugar	1 cup	170g	6oz
Butter/margarine/lard	1 cup	225g	8oz
Sultanas/raisins	1 cup	200g	7oz
Currants	1 cup	140g	5oz
Ground almonds	1 cup	110g	4oz
Golden syrup	1 cup	340g	12oz
Butter	1 stick	110g	4oz

Liquid measures

Imperial	ml	fl oz
1¾ pints	1000 (1 litre)	35
1 pint	570	20
¾ pint	425	15
½ pint	290	10
⅓ pint	190	6.6
¼ pint (1 gill)	150	5
4 scant tablespoons	56	
2 scant tablespoons	28	
1 teaspoon	5	

Australian

250ml	1 cup
20ml	1 tablespoon
5ml	1 teaspoon

Approximate American/European conversions

American	European
10 pints	4.5 litres/8 pints
2½ pints (5 cups)	1.1 litres/2 pints
1 pint/16fl oz	1 pint/20fl oz/5.75ml
1¼ cups	½ pint/10fl oz/290ml
½ cup plus 2 tablespoons	¼ pint/5fl oz/150ml
¼ cup	4 tablespoons/2fl oz/55ml
½fl oz	1 tablespoon/½fl oz/15ml
1 teaspoon	1 teaspoon/5ml

Useful measurements

Measurement	Metric	Imperial
1 American cup	225ml	8fl oz
1 egg, size 3	56ml	2fl oz
1 egg white	28ml	1fl oz
1 rounded tablespoon flour	30g	1oz
1 rounded tablespoon cornflour	30g	1oz
1 rounded tablespoon caster sugar	30g	1oz
2 rounded tablespoons fresh breadcrumbs	30g	1oz

Lengths

Imperial	Metric
½in	1cm
1in	2.5cm
2in	5cm
6in	15cm
12in	30cm

Oven temperatures

°C	°F	Gas mark	AMERICAN	AUSTRALIAN
70	150	¼		
80	175	¼	COOL	VERY SLOW
100	200	½		
110	225	½		
130	250	1	VERY SLOW	
140	275	1		SLOW
150	300	2	SLOW	
170	325	3	MODERATE	MODERATELY SLOW
180	350	4		
190	375	5	MODERATELY HOT	MODERATE
200	400	6	FAIRLY HOT	
220	425	7	HOT	MODERATELY HOT
230	450	8	VERY HOT	
240	475	8		HOT
250	500	9		
270	525	9	EXTREMELY HOT	
290	550	9		VERY HOT

LEITH'S BOOK OF CAKES

CAKE MAKING

Knowledgeable cake-makers are able to adapt recipes or alter ingredients, but the novice or less experienced cook should stick rigidly to the recipe. Careful weighing and measuring, using the correct utensils and equipment, not rushing the process, precise oven temperatures and careful timing will ensure good results. For those new to cake-making it is best to start with the easier cakes such as gingerbread, fruit cake or rock cakes.

Most cakes are made by mixing fat, sugar, flour, eggs and liquid together. The mixture rises during baking through the inclusion of air or other raising agents such as baking powder which will form carbon dioxide gas. As the cake bakes, strands of a protein called gluten, present in the flour, are stretched by the gas given off until the heat cooks and firms the cake.

Before you start to make the cake, always weigh all the ingredients to ensure you have enough of each one, preheat the oven and prepare the cake tin.

Methods

Rubbing in

The fat and flour are rubbed together with the fingertips as for pastry. The raising agent will usually be self-raising flour, baking powder or bicarbonate of soda. The resulting cake has a very crumbly texture, for example rock cakes.

Melting

The fat, sugar and syrup are heated gently in a saucepan and then allowed to cool slightly. The flour and other dry ingredients are sifted together and the cooled melted mixture plus any other liquid, for example milk and eggs, are stirred in carefully. The raising agent is bicarbonate of soda. These cakes are easy to make and are very moist, for example gingerbread. They have very good keeping qualities.

Creaming

Fat and sugar are beaten together to form a creamy consistency. Air is incorporated and together with self-raising flour and eggs makes a light sponge which will keep well in a tin for a week. The creaming method is also used for many rich fruit cakes.

When the eggs are added to the creamed butter and sugar they must be incorporated slowly or the mixture will curdle. If there are signs that this may happen, adding a tablespoon of flour will solve the problem. However, if the mixture does curdle the result will be a cake that is coarser in texture but still acceptable.

A creamed cake mixture ready to bake is often described in recipes as 'of dropping consistency'. This means that the mixture will fall off the spoon rather reluctantly and in a single blob. If it runs off it is too wet, and if it will not fall off even when the spoon is jerked slightly, it is too dry.

'All-in-one' cakes are an adaptation of creamed cakes. All the ingredients are beaten together with a strong electric mixer. You must ensure the butter is soft before it is used, or use a soft tub margarine.

Boiling

This is an old-fashioned method used for fruit cakes. It does not mean the cake itself is boiled rather than baked but that some of the ingredients are brought to the boil together prior to baking. Usually butter, sugar, dried fruit and any liquid are brought to the boil and then allowed to cool before any other ingredients are added. Sometimes they will be left to soak together for a couple of days before completing. Then the eggs, flour and spices are simply stirred in. This method produces a very rich cake with wonderfully plump fruit, which has very good keeping qualities.

Yeast

Many European-style cakes are made using yeast. They usually have a high butter, sugar and fruit content. Because both butter and sugar affect the rising effect (proving) of the yeast, the texture of these cakes will be both closer and softer than that of bread. The mixture often takes a long time to rise or prove, but does so quickly once put into the oven. Examples of cakes using yeast are Gugelhopf, Panettone and Stollen.

Whisking

The eggs and sugar are whisked together, sometimes over heat, until the mixture is thick and light. The raising agent is the trapped air which causes the cake to rise in the heat of the oven.

The simplest whisked sponge contains no fat. Sifted flour is gently folded into the whisked eggs and sugar so that as much air as possible is retained. For a genoise, some melted, but not hot, butter is folded into the mixture. In a lighter but more complicated whisked sponge, the eggs are separated and the whites are whisked in a separate bowl, with a little sugar added to make a meringue. This is then folded into the yolks and flour to make a more stable mixture.

If the mixture is underwhisked, the cake will not rise sufficiently. If it is overwhisked the cake will be tough. Folding in the flour is important too: if overfolded, the incorporated air will escape, resulting in a flat cake; if underfolded, pockets of flour will remain and spoil the finished cake.

Occasionally whisked sponges include a little baking powder to ensure success but a classic whisked sponge or genoise has only the whisked-in, trapped air as its raising agent.

Whisked sponges are light and springy but they go stale quickly. A genoise, because of the addition of butter, will keep for a day or two longer. Both cakes freeze very successfully (see page 32,35).

To test when a cake is cooked

When checking whether a cake is done, do the test while the cake is still in the oven, and test as quickly as possible. If a cake is removed from the oven before it is ready it will sink in the middle.

A sponge cake is ready when the sides have shrunk away slightly from the tin and the cake feels firm to the touch and springs back when pressed lightly with a fingertip.

A rich fruit cake is ready when the top feels firm to the touch and when a sharp knife or skewer inserted at an angle into the centre of the cake comes out clean. The knife or skewer will be moist when the cake is cooked but it should not have any uncooked mixture on it.

A yeast-risen cake is ready when it sounds hollow when tapped on the underside.

Cooling cakes

Most cakes benefit from being left to cool in the tin for a few minutes before they are turned out. This helps to prevent the possibility of their collapsing. However, sponge cakes will become soggy if they are left to cool completely in the tin and should be turned out on to a wire rack after 5–10 minutes.

Rich fruit cakes should be cooled completely in the tin as they are heavy, and fragile when hot. Placing the tin on a wire rack will speed up the cooling process. Yeast cakes and cakes, biscuits and buns cooked on a baking sheet should be removed immediately they come out of the oven and placed on a wire rack to cool.

Turning out cakes

If a cake tin is properly greased and lined (see page 29–30) there should be no problem with turning out. With sponge cakes, after the initial cooling in the tin run a round-bladed knife carefully around the edge, avoiding cutting into the crust. Invert the tin and turn the cake out, then quickly but carefully peel off the disc of lining paper and put the cake the right way up (crust side on top) on to a wire rack.

A rich fruit cake can be left in its lining paper after turning out, if it is to be stored for any length of time.

A cake baked in a moule à manqué tin is always served upside-down (with the crust on the bottom).

A cake baked in a loose-bottomed tin can be removed by placing the tin on top of a container of a smaller diameter. The sides of the tin will fall down leaving the cake on the base. Then simply remove the base from the cake with the aid of a palette knife.

A spring-form tin has a clip on the side which when unclipped loosens the sides of the tin away from the cake, making it easy to lift off. The base is then removed with the aid of a palette knife.

In most cases if a cake is to be cooled quickly the lining paper can be removed immediately but it will not matter if it is left on until the cake is cold.

Splitting a cake into layers

Some recipes require a single cake to be split into 2 or 3 layers before sandwiching together with a filling. This can be tricky if the cake is thin and fragile. The following points should help to achieve neat and even layers.

1. Use a large bread knife or serrated edged knife.

2. Place the cake on a board or flat surface (not a plate).

3. Make 2 or 3 incisions horizontally into

the cake ensuring that they are spaced evenly apart.

4. If cutting the cake into 3 layers, start with the top cut. Place your hand flat on the surface of the cake and using the centre of the blade of the knife cut through very carefully with a sawing action. Do not turn the cake around as you work. Lift off the top layer and repeat with a second cut.

5. Reassemble the cake until ready to use with the layers in their original order so that the cake is even and flat on top.

Freezing and storing cakes

Most of the cakes in this book will freeze well. However, if an iced cake is frozen, the icing can weep a little when it defrosts. It is not advisable to freeze cakes covered with fondant icing or royal icing. Cakes with glacé icing can be frozen but they will lose their glossy streak and not look quite as good once they have defrosted.

Rich fruit cakes wrapped and stored in an airtight tin keep perfectly well and so do not require freezing but sponge cakes which stale quickly can be frozen. Generally cakes made using the melting method (see page 14) will improve with keeping and will keep in an airtight container for up to 2 weeks. They will also freeze very successfully.

Any cake that is to be frozen can be open-frozen first, that is, placed in the freezer uncovered. Once the cake has frozen it must be put into a freezer bag, wrapped in kitchen foil or placed in a polythene freezer box. It should be well wrapped to prevent the cold air in the freezer getting to it and causing freezer burn. All cakes can be kept in the freezer for up to 3 months, after which they will start to become dry.

Ingredients
Flour

Wheat grains produce the best flour for cake-making. This is because when it is mixed with water or other liquids, a complex protein, called gluten, is formed, which helps the mixture to rise and set. In other grains these proteins are either of an inferior quality or are absent altogether. The gluten forms an elastic structure throughout the cake mixture. Water is trapped between the strands of gluten and as the cake is baked in the oven, this evaporates as steam. This steam, along with the help of the air which has been beaten in (or another raising agent, such as baking powder), lifts and rises the cake. The heat of the oven causes the mixture to set firmly.

Different types of wheat yield different amounts of gluten. For breads and risen pastries such as puff pastry, strong flour, which is high in gluten, is used. This will give a strong, firm texture. For cakes, however, less gluten is required, and so an ordinary plain flour is used.

Various ingredients are included in cake mixtures and bread doughs to either strengthen or soften the gluten. This is why cakes, breads, yeast-risen cakes and pastries will have slightly different textures even when the same flour is used.

Ingredients which strengthen gluten
water
salt
acid, such as lemon juice

The handling of the dough, for example kneading or beating, also helps the dough to rise.

Ingredients which soften gluten

fat, such as butter, oil, eggs, whole cream milk
sugar
bran in flour
enzymes in yeast

In North America, plain or 'all purpose' flour is made with more hard than soft wheat, so cornflour, which is 'weak' (low in gluten), is sometimes substituted for some of the all-purpose flour, or a special soft cake flour is used.

Self-raising flour is plain flour with a raising agent (baking powder) added to it, and should be used only if specified in the recipe. If you need to turn plain flour into self-raising flour, add 3 teaspoons baking powder to 225g/8oz plain flour.

Fats

Fats have the effect of shortening the cake mixture. This means that when the fat is distributed throughout the mixture it shortens the strands of gluten and so produces a much softer result which is more crumbly and 'melts in the mouth'.

Butter gives the best flavour to cakes. It should be used softened, but not melted, for creamed cakes. In this way the fat will hold air.

Margarine, particularly the soft or tub variety, can be used for speed and is also cheaper, but it doesn't have the flavour of butter. Vegetable shortenings are flavourless but give a lighter result.

Lard produces a crumbly and soft result which is delicious but tends to be heavy. It is very rarely used in cakes but there are some notable exceptions such as Lardy Cake. Lard is also the best fat to use for greasing tins (see page 29).

Oil is sometimes used in cakes, particularly in American recipes. It can give a very soft result with a distinctive flavour but the cakes are often very heavy as it is difficult to get the oil to hold air when it is beaten.

Eggs

Unless otherwise specified, the recipes in this book assume a medium egg (UK size 3). Eggs, when beaten with sugar, help the cake to rise. Sponges made by this method are usually very light. However, when the cake does not include enough egg to make it rise, some form of chemical raising agent is necessary.

Eggs should be used at room temperature. If used straight from the refrigerator, they have a tendency to curdle the mixture which will give the cake a tough, coarse texture.

If whisked egg whites are used in a cake, do not allow even a speck of yolk or grease into the white. This will prevent the proper whisking of the whites which will reduce their air-holding capacity and the lightness of the finished cake. Egg whites can be whisked to different stages as specified in the recipe.
Soft peak: the egg white just about holds its shape but when the whisk is lifted out of the mixture the peaks will collapse. This is the stage for folding into a very thick mixture.
Medium peak: when the whisk is lifted out of the mixture the tops of the peaks will flop over a little. This is the most common stage used for cakes and soufflés.
Stiff peak: when the egg white holds its shape and the peaks formed by the whisk stand up stiffly. This is the stage used for meringues and some cakes.

When folding in egg whites use the largest

metal spoon available, add a tablespoon of the whisked egg white to the mixture and stir it in. This loosens the mixture so that it will more readily accept the remaining egg white which should be folded in as quickly as possible with a figure-of-eight movement. Overfolding will cause the cake to lose bulk.

Sugars

Caster sugar is best for creamed cakes. It produces a lighter texture than granulated sugar which can give a speckled appearance to the finished cake. However, granulated sugar can be used if ground down in a blender or food processor first.

Soft brown sugar (light or dark, depending on the molasses content) gives colour and flavour to cakes such as gingerbreads or rich fruit cakes but would give a sponge cake a taste of caramel. Soft dark brown sugar has a stronger flavour than light.

Muscovado sugar (also available light or dark) is made from unrefined (raw) cane sugar and has a fine flavour.

Cakes made by the melting method are often sweetened with golden syrup, treacle, molasses or honey instead of sugar. They are baked quite slowly as they can caramelize and burn at high temperatures.

Raising agents

Beating butter and sugar together, whisking eggs, or sifting flour, incorporates air into the cake mixture. The heat of the oven causes the air trapped in the mixture to expand and the steam produced by the moisture also causes the cake to rise. Steam rises some mixtures even when air has not

been beaten in.

When there is not enough natural leavening in a cake, a chemical leavening can be used. This will produce carbon dioxide gas which will expand during baking. The most common type of commercial raising agent is baking powder. This is a mixture of bicarbonate of soda and an acid such as cream of tartar, usually with a starch filler such as cornflour, ground rice, arrowroot or wheat flour. This helps to keep the mixture dry by absorbing any moisture in the air which might cause the bicarbonate of soda and acid to react.

Once a chemical leavening is added to the cake mixture you must work quickly or the gas will escape from the mixture before the cake is put into the oven. A delayed action, or double action, baking powder, sold in the USA, needs heat as well as moisture to produce carbon dioxide. It is not widely used in Europe but the advantage is that it will not start working until it is put into the oven. Too much raising agent will not only impair the flavour of the cake but will result in a cracked peak forming on top.

Bicarbonate of soda is sometimes used alone, when there are other ingredients in the cake mixture which will cause it to give off carbon dioxide. These include sour milk, buttermilk, vinegar, soured cream, cream of tartar, yoghurt, and the natural acids in honey, treacle and fresh milk. Once the cake is set and cooked by heat the carbon dioxide is replaced by air as it cools. The bicarbonate of soda left in the cake, particularly if too much is used in the first place, can give an unpleasant smell and taste as well as an orangey-yellow colour. For this reason cakes that use bicarbonate of soda are usually strong-tasting ones such as gingerbreads flavoured with chocolate, treacle or molasses.

Yeast

Yeast is used in some cakes as a raising agent. It is particularly popular in Germanic or Eastern European cakes which are really sweetened, enriched breads.

Yeast is a fungus and is a single-celled organism. In order to reproduce, it needs a combination of food (sugar or starch), warmth and moisture.

If yeast is given too much heat in the early stage it can be killed off before it has a chance to reproduce. Conversely, if the temperature is too low it can become dormant. For this reason yeast dough can usefully be refrigerated to stop it rising further, until it is convenient to bake it. However, the dough will need to be brought to room temperature first, to re-activate the yeast.

Once the yeast is activated, the cells will start to divide by splitting in half (binary fission). By-products of this activity are alcohol and carbon dioxide gas. The alcohol gives the familiar beery, yeasty smell and the carbon dioxide becomes trapped within the dough to form a spongy, mesh-like structure during the process known as rising or proving. When the dough is put into the oven the yeast is killed by the heat and the alcohol is burnt off.

The best type of yeast to use is compressed fresh yeast. It is dependable, rises well and gives a better flavour to the finished dough. It is available at the bakery counter of some supermarkets, in bakeries where baking is carried out on the premises and in health food shops. It must be kept refrigerated and will keep for approximately 2 weeks. It can be frozen but only for about 1 month. Freeze it in usable quantities and use it from frozen as when it defrosts it turns to liquid.

The alternative to fresh yeast is active dry yeast, which should be date-stamped. When using dry yeast use half the amount of fresh yeast mentioned in the recipe. Dry yeast is activated by mixing with a little sugar or flour and warm liquid. The mixture is then left to 'sponge'. A frothy foam should appear on the surface. When it does, the yeast is ready to use. If it doesn't, the yeast is dead and should be thrown away.

Easy-blend yeast is sprinkled directly on to the flour and when the liquid is added the yeast starts to activate. It is best to follow the directions on the packet.

All types of yeast can be inhibited in their rising by too much salt, sugar or fat.

Other Ingredients and Flavourings

Chocolate

Chocolate is produced from cocoa beans. These are harvested from the large pods which grow on cocoa trees in Central and South America and West Africa. The beans and pulp are scraped from the pods and fermented in the sun for a few days. The pulp evaporates and the beans change in colour from pale violet to dark brown. The beans are then sun-dried prior to being exported, when they are processed further. The cocoa beans are roasted, removed from their husks and ground. The grinding process produces heat which melts the fat (cocoa butter) away from the beans. The resulting thick, sticky mixture is a crude form of bitter chocolate, called cocoa liquor or cocoa solids, from which cocoa powder and more refined chocolates are prepared.

The higher the cocoa solid content, the more intense the flavour of the chocolate.

Bitter, dark chocolate contains 75 per cent cocoa solids and no added sugar. It is very rich.

Chocolate couverture also contains a high proportion of cocoa solids. To make it shiny and glossy it should be tempered (melted to the correct temperature, quickly cooled down and then reheated) before use to make it easier to work with. It is available plain, milk or white.

Plain chocolate contains 30–60 per cent cocoa solids and sugar. The higher the percentage of cocoa solids, the richer the flavour will be.

Milk chocolate contains approximately 35 per cent cocoa solids, sugar and milk. It has a tendency to seize when melted, unless this is done very carefully.

White chocolate contains approximately 25 per cent cocoa butter, sugar and milk. It has no cocoa solids, hence its colour. It is the most difficult chocolate to use in cooking and care must be taken when melting it.

Chocolate flavoured cake covering is made from vegetable oil, sugar flavourings and cocoa and has a tendency to leave a fatty film in the mouth. It is not recommended for the recipes in this book.

Cocoa powder is made when cocoa butter is extracted from the cocoa solids. The block that is left is ground to a powder. It is used in cakes and biscuits because it is easier to work with than chocolate and gives a very strong, bitter flavour. However, it does not have the richness of chocolate.

Chocolate chips or buttons are available in plain, milk and white chocolate. They are easy to weigh exactly and melt quickly. They are also useful if a recipe calls for chocolate chunks or pieces.

Chocolate caraque: these are thin rolls of chocolate for decorating cakes and gâteaux. To make caraque, melt 100g/4oz plain chocolate carefully, then pour on to a cold work surface (a slab of marble is ideal). Allow to cool and harden. Take a large sharp kitchen knife and scrape it across the surface of the sheet of chocolate, making a cigar-shaped roll. Repeat until all the chocolate is used up. If the chocolate splinters as you work, this means that the chocolate is too cold and it should be moved to a warmer temperature. Caraque can be stored for a short time in an airtight container in a cool place.

Dried Fruits

Dried fruits are produced from ripe fresh fruit and are classified into two groups: vine fruits and tree fruits. The moisture content is reduced by drying and the fruits change character completely, becoming dense, wrinkled and leathery. The flavour is sweet and very concentrated. Approximately 1.8–2.3kg/4–5lb fresh grapes will produce 450g/1lb sultanas, raisins or currants, whereas 2.7kg/6lb tree fruit will produce about 450g/1lb dried tree fruit.

Dried fruit is often treated with sulphur to keep the colour and to extend its shelf life. Fruit that has been treated will be labelled as such and will keep for 18 months in a cool, well-ventilated dry place. Once a packet has been opened the fruit should be kept in an airtight container.

Dried fruit is higher in calories than fresh fruit but is a very good source of dietary fibre and is nutritious. It contains a lot of fruit sugars – fructose and glucose – and therefore provides a constant source of energy.

Vine Fruits

Vine fruits account for three-quarters of total dried fruit production.

Sultanas: Mainly produced in Turkey, Australia, Greece, Iran and South Africa, largely from seedless white grapes. They are amber-coloured and have a very sweet flavour. The majority are produced from the Thompson seedless grape which contains 18–20 per cent fruit sugar. This helps to retain a plump fruit after evaporation of its water content. There are different methods of drying sultanas, depending on country of origin. One way is to spray the grapes with a vegetable-based drying oil prior to sun-drying. This will make the water evaporate more quickly from the fruit when exposed to the sun. In some places the fruit is dried on racks in partial shade whilst in other countries the fruit is put in full sun on specially shaped concrete drying areas. Drying takes a week to 10 days until the moisture is reduced to approximately 16 per cent. The fruit is processed in factories where it is washed, cleaned and given a fine coating of vegetable oil. This keeps the sultanas moist and prevents them from sticking together.

Raisins: Mainly produced in California, South Africa, Afghanistan, Chile and Australia, from unseeded or seeded black or white grapes. The word raisin is derived from the Latin, *racemus*, which means 'a cluster of grapes or berries'. Raisins are generally dark brown and wrinkled, with a sweet, mellow flavour. The grapes are harvested when fully ripened and, as for sultanas, they are dried by different methods depending on the country of origin. Sometimes the grapes are dried on clean paper trays between the vines or are placed in specially made concrete drying areas. The clusters of grapes are spread out evenly and turned occasionally so that each grape gets the right amount of sun. The fruit lies in full sunlight for 2–3 weeks until the moisture content has been reduced to around 16 per cent. They are then packed into storage bins to keep them moist and are washed and oiled before export.

Currants: 95 per cent are produced in Greece and the remainder in South Africa, Australia and the USA. Currants are dried black seedless grapes. They all derive from the same type, the Corinth, and this is where the name currant originated. The methods of drying vary depending on the climate and soil of the growing area. But it is said that keeping the grapes in the shade for the first stage of the drying process will produce the best-quality currant. Currants are graded into two sizes: small and medium. The small ones are used by the baking industry whereas the currants available in grocery and health food shops are generally the medium-sized variety.

Tree Fruits

Dried tree fruits have become increasingly popular and more widely available. They are very versatile and, apart from their use in cakes, they can also be reconstituted and used as purées or sauces and to accompany meat dishes, or as puddings in their own right. Generally they do not need soaking for use in cakes, but when being used for a pudding or as a sauce they will need to be soaked and/or cooked.

The most common and widely available dried tree fruits are:

Apples: Available peeled, cored and sliced into rings or chunks.

Apricots: Available halved or whole. They are usually bright orange, but the unsulphured variety is dark brown. The small Hunza apricot is beige and has a very sweet, slightly caramel flavour when eaten unsoaked. They are grown in the wild in the valleys of Afghanistan and Kashmir. Many of the dried apricots found in the shops come from Turkey.

Dates: Available whole or in blocks with the stones removed. They grow on the date palm.

Figs: Available whole or in blocks. Dried figs are sweet and pale yellow-brown in colour. Apart from giving sweetness and richness to a cake, they also lend a slightly gritty texture.

Peaches: Available in either halves or slices, they have a slightly sharp, tangy flavour and can give a traditional fruit cake a wonderful edge.

Pears: Available in halves, they are a golden-yellow colour with a granular texture.

Prunes: Available whole or pitted. Prunes are dark dried plums and like most tree fruits give extra moistness to a cake.

Other dried tree fruits available include nectarines, mangoes, bananas, paw paw, cherries and cranberries.

Glacé Fruits

Glacé fruits are preserved by cooking and soaking (macerating) in a strong sugar syrup.

They are time-consuming to make at home as they take several weeks to complete. Glacé cherries are most commonly used in cakes. The variety most often seen are bright red, having been dyed to produce a rather unnatural colour. Undyed ones are also available and are a much darker red. Yellow and green (dyed) glacé cherries are useful for decoration, as in the Old-fashioned Boiled Christmas Cake (see page 51).

Mixed peel is a mixture of glacéed or crystallized orange, lemon and lime peel. It is commonly available in diced form. More expensively glacéed and crystallized citrus peel – lemon, orange, lime and grapefruit – is available in large pieces which have a far superior flavour to commercial chopped mixed peel.

Making your own crystallized peel at home will take about a month from start to finish, but the result will have a wonderful fresh flavour and will be much more economical than shop-bought peel. Use the peel of 6 oranges, lemons, limes or grapefruit, or a mixture of the four, and 370g/12oz granulated sugar. Wash the fruit well, peel and cut the peel into quarters. Cover with water in a saucepan and simmer for 1½–2 hours until quite tender. (If using grapefruit, change the water twice.) Strain the liquid and make up to 290ml/½ pint with water. Return the liquid to the pan, add 225g/8oz of the sugar and heat gently until the sugar has dissolved. Bring to the boil and add the peel, then remove from the heat, transfer to a bowl, cover and leave to macerate for 2 days in a cool place.

Drain the syrup into a saucepan, add the remaining sugar and dissolve carefully. Bring to the boil, add the peel and simmer over a low heat for about 20–30 minutes or until the peel is semi-transparent. Pour into a bowl, allow to cool, cover and leave in a cool place for 2–3 weeks.

Remove the peel from the syrup, place on a wire rack and leave to dry out in an airing cupboard or other warm place where the temperature does not exceed 50°C/120°F. When the peel has lost its stickiness, store with waxed paper between the layers in a cardboard or wooden, not polythene, box. For a crystallized finish, dip the peel in boiling water briefly, drain thoroughly and roll in caster sugar. Leave to dry, then chop and use as required.

Small amounts of glacé fruit in a cake mixture, such as in Cherry Cake (see page 45), have a tendency to sink to the bottom during baking. To avoid this, wash off the syrup, dry thoroughly and coat with flour before adding to the mixture.

Fresh Fruits

Fresh fruits such as apples, pears, plums, peaches, pineapple, rhubarb, etc., can be added to cake recipes but as they produce a lot of moisture when they cook, the addition of too much would make the cake soggy.

Vegetables

Vegetables such as carrots, potatoes, sweet potatoes, pumpkin, parsnips, courgettes, etc., are sometimes included in cakes, particularly American-style cakes, to add extra texture, moisture and flavour. Carrots and parsnips, for example, have a great deal of natural sweetness which they can give to a cake. They are usually included in a recipe either raw and grated or cooked and puréed.

Nuts

Nuts are the fruit of various types of tree, and many different types can be used in cake-making. Most are now available all year round, although some are seasonal, such as chestnuts. Nuts that are available fresh are referred to as 'green'. Most are dried, which means that they have a longer shelf life. They go off quickly, so it is best to buy them in small quantities and store them for a short time. Stale nuts will taste rancid and bitter.

When buying unshelled nuts, avoid any with damp and mouldy shells as they can contain toxins. Nuts should feel heavy for their size. The more processed the nuts, the quicker they will go off. Thus almonds in their shells will have a longer shelf life than ground, blanched almonds.

Nuts are a good source of energy as they are high in protein, carbohydrate and fat. This means that they tend to be very high in calories, except for chestnuts, which are low-fat.

Many nuts are grown for their oil as well as their value as a nut meat. These include, particularly, hazelnuts, walnuts, peanuts and almonds.

The flavour of nuts is always improved if they are roasted for a few minutes before being used.

Almonds: The almond is related to the plum, peach and apricot. Almonds are grown commercially in many different parts of the world including California, Australia, North Africa, Spain, Italy and Portugal. There are two types, sweet and bitter. The most generally available are the sweet variety. Bitter almonds are poisonous if eaten raw but the toxins are destroyed by heat when cooked.

Almond kernels can be used with the skin on, as in praline, or can be blanched in boiling water. The skin will rub off after a few minutes. Almonds are generally used in cakes whole, flaked, nibbed or ground. They are probably the most-used nut in cake-making and form the base of marzipan. Ground almonds are sometimes used in place of flour to make moist cakes or biscuits such as macaroons.

Brazil nuts: Brazil nuts are grown mainly in Brazil and neighbouring countries. They are very high in fat and therefore go rancid quite quickly. They are large and fleshy and can be used chopped or grated in cakes, and whole as part of decorative toppings.

Sweet chestnuts: Chestnuts are grown in areas of temperate climate. The sweet chestnut is encased in a green, prickly outer skin. Unlike most nuts, chestnuts bought in their shells are always in their fresh, undried state. Because of this they should be eaten quickly.

To prepare chestnuts, prick the shells and put them into a moderate oven for 10–15 minutes. (Failure to prick the shell will cause the nut to explode, which can be very dangerous.) Remove from the oven and allow to cool slightly. Peel off the shell, beneath which the chestnuts are covered with a brown skin. To remove this, blanch the shelled nuts in boiling water for a couple of minutes and then pick off the skin, which is a very fiddly job. Ready-shelled and skinned chestnuts are available in vacuum packs. They are mostly used in cakes in a sweetened purée form (available tinned) and combine particularly well with chocolate. Chestnut flour, which is used in Indian, Corsican, Italian and Spanish cooking, is also available from health food shops and specialist food stores.

Coconut: Coconut for use in cake-making is generally grated or desiccated. Grated fresh coconut is particularly good in cakes and biscuits. Desiccated coconut is dried, grated fresh coconut and will lose its flavour if it is stored for too long.

Hazelnuts: Also known as Barcelona nuts, cobnuts, filberts or Kentish cobnuts. Turkey is the largest producer of hazelnuts, but the USA, Italy and Spain also export them.

To remove the skins from shelled hazelnuts, roast them in a moderate oven for 10 minutes, then rub them in a clean tea towel. Once they have been roasted they should not be stored for very long. In cakes, hazelnuts are used whole, chopped or ground.

Macadamia nuts: Native to the woodlands of Australia but also grown in California, Hawaii and Latin America. The shells are incredibly hard to crack and the nuts are round, white and quite high in fat. They are expensive but give a special richness to cakes and biscuits and a few go a long way.

Peanuts: Also known as the groundnut or monkey nut, the peanut is not actually a nut, but a legume, a member of the pea and bean family, and grows underground. Peanuts are very versatile and can be used, whole or chopped, in cakes, or as peanut butter. Groundnut or arachide oil is derived from peanuts.

Walnuts: Walnuts are used in a large variety of cakes and biscuits. They need to be used quickly as rancid walnuts have a very bitter flavour. They combine well with other flavours, particularly coffee, orange and chocolate.

Bakeware

Cake tins

Cake tins should be strong and of a good weight. This prevents them from buckling in the heat of the oven and ensures that the heat is evenly conducted to the cake. Most cake tins are made of aluminium: the thicker the metal, the better the quality. Silicone non-stick tins are expensive but probably the best of the non-stick range and a worthwhile investment. Care should be taken when loosening cakes in these tins with a knife, so as not to scratch the surface.

Some of the tins mentioned below, e.g. sandwich tins and deep cake tins, are available loose-bottomed. These are particularly useful for fragile cakes and cakes that cannot be turned out by inverting the tin, such as Squashy Rhubarb Cake (see page 64).

Size as specified in the recipe is critical. If the cake tin is too big the mixture will cook unevenly and too fast. If it is too small the mixture may cook too slowly, develop an uneven texture, overflow or burn on the top whilst remaining uncooked inside. Tins should be between half and two-thirds full before baking.

Sandwich tin: This is a shallow tin and 2 of the same size are generally required. For a 2-egg Victoria sandwich you will need 2 × 15cm/6in tins; for a 3-egg sponge 2 × 18cm/7in tins, and so on.

Deep cake tin (round or square): Often used for fruit cakes. Heavy duty tins are best as often these cakes are baked at a low oven temperature and for a long time. It is useful to have 2 different sizes about 7.5cm/3in deep.

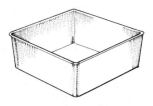

Moule-à-manqué: A traditional French sponge tin used for whisked sponges and genoise. It has sloping sides and the cake is served upside-down.

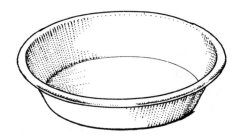

Springform tin: The base is separate from the sides, which have a clip to loosen them. These tins, which are useful for large, more delicate cakes, are often sold with an extra base with a funnel in it.

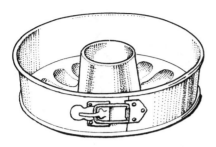

Bun or patty tins: These usually contain 12 moulds, not all of which need to be filled. Useful for small cakes or tartlets. Muffin tins have deeper moulds.

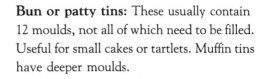

Loaf tin: Available in various sizes, these tins have sloping sides to give a larger surface area.

Swiss roll tin: This is usually 2.5cm/1in high and about 35 × 25cm/14 × 10in. It should be reasonably heavy duty as otherwise the heat of the oven will make it buckle and the cake's thickness will be uneven.

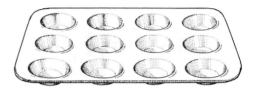

Baking sheet: It is advisable to have a few of these in different sizes. Lipless ones are good if the article being baked is fragile and needs to be slid off rather than lifted. Lipped baking sheets are useful where there is a chance of overflow. Sides bigger than 1cm/½in inhibit the flow of air. Large baking sheets should be at least 2.5cm/1in smaller than the oven all the way round.

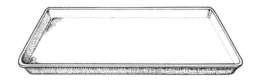

Fluted flan tin: Available in many different sizes. They vary in depth and are best if made of strong metal with a removable base.

Gugelhopf mould or tin: This has a patterned edge and a funnel in the centre to allow the heat to reach the centre of the cake. This tin can also be used for Angel cakes.

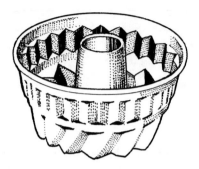

Cake rack or cooling rack: A large rack is most useful. It should be strong and 1–2.5cm/½–1in high to allow the air to circulate underneath to cool the baked cakes effectively. A circular rack is ideal for cooling larger, heavier cakes as they are less likely to sag in the middle.

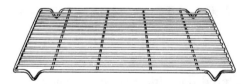

Pastry cutters: These can be bought in sets and should have the top edge rolled to keep the shape rigid and to ensure your fingers don't get cut. They are available with plain or fluted edges.

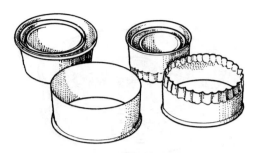

Pastry brush: This should be of good quality with tightly packed bristles which will not shed. It is useful to have 2 or 3.

Icing bags: Nylon bags with sewn seams will last longer than plastic ones. The bags vary in size and it is useful to have a selection of different sizes. These bags can be boiled. For royal icing it is easier to make your own greaseproof bags (see pages 149–51).

Icing pipes (nozzles): The best icing pipes are made of strong stainless steel and are less likely to buckle or lose their shape. Metal pipes give a better definition than plastic. Most makes have numbers on each pipe which signifies the type. As good-quality pipes are expensive, it is advisable to build up a collection gradually. The most useful are writing pipes (thin, medium, thick) and star pipes (small, medium, large). Ribbon and petal pipes are useful once you have become more adept at icing.

Icing turntable: In general the more you spend on this the better it will be. To ice the heavy bottom tier of a wedding cake it is important to have a strong, stable and sturdy turntable which will turn smoothly and easily. This will also serve for any other cake.

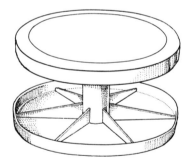

Cake boards: Cake boards should be 5cm/2in bigger than the cake, with the exception of the bottom tier of a wedding cake which should have a cake board 10cm/4in bigger. Boards can be iced once the cake has been base-iced. The icing will need to be a little thinner than for the cake and once it has been iced do not move the cake until the icing is dry otherwise it will crack. The sides of the board can be covered with ribbon.

Cake pillars: The best cake pillars are made from plaster of paris. Both square and round pillars are available from specialist cake shops and are usually 7.5cm/3in high. Eight pillars are normally required for a 3-tier cake: 4 for each tier or 5 to support the middle tier and 3 to support the top tier. When designing the decoration for the cake, bear in mind where the pillars are to be placed.

Preparing a Cake Tin

All tins, even non-stick ones, should be greased to prevent the cake mixture from sticking or burning round the sides or on the base. Melted lard is the best fat to use for greasing as it is cleaner and less likely to stick. Vegetable oil can be used more easily but it does tend to leave a yellow, sticky deposit on the cake tin which needs to be well cleaned to avoid build-up. Butter is sometimes suggested to help form a crust on the sides of the cake, but it is expensive to use and unnecessary for most cakes.

Always melt solid fats before using for greasing because then much less will be required and it will form a more even layer. Thickly greased cake tins have a tendency to 'fry' the cakes on the outside crust. Use a pastry brush or a piece of absorbent paper dipped into the fat or oil to get a thin layer.

Bread tins just need to be greased although it is occasionally suggested that the tins are dusted with flour as well.

Creamed cakes or melting method cakes should be put into tins which have been greased and the base lined with a piece of greased greaseproof paper, cut to fit. To cut the paper accurately, draw round the tin and cut just inside the line.

Whisked cakes are put into tins which have been greased and lined as above and then dusted with a layer of caster sugar and flour.

For fruit cakes and other cakes that are to be baked for a long time and need extra protection, line the base and sides with greaseproof paper as follows:

1. Cut 2 pieces of greaseproof paper to fit the base of the cake tin.
2. Cut another 2 pieces long enough to go right round the sides of the tin and to overlap slightly. They should be 3.5cm/1½in deeper than the height of the cake tin.
3. Place one long strip on top of the other and fold one long edge of this double strip over 2.5cm/1in all along its length.
4. Cut snips at 45° angles from the edge to the folded line about 1cm/1½in apart all along the long folded side. The snips should just reach the fold.
5. Grease the tin with melted lard or oil, place one paper base in the bottom and grease again.
6. Fit the long strip inside the tin with the folded cut edge on the bottom (the flanges should overlap slightly) and the main uncut part lining the sides of the tin. Press well into the base (and corners if using a square tin).
7. Grease the paper and lay the second base on top of the first and over the flanges of paper.
8. Brush the base again with more melted lard or oil.
9. Once the cake mixture is in the tin it is wise to wrap several layers of newspaper around the outside of the tin and secure with string. The newspaper should come 2.5cm/1in above the top of the tin. This extra wrapping may mean that the cake will take longer to bake but it will be less likely to burn.

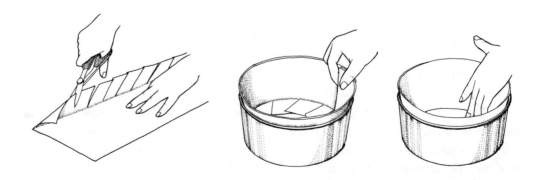

1 CLASSIC CAKES

This section is made up of classic, basic recipes, some more elaborate ones for special occasions, and a selection of old favourites. It is impossible to include every classic cake, but these are the best! Some classic recipes can also be found elsewhere in the book, for example Dundee Cake in the Fruit Cakes chapter.

♦ ♦

Victoria Sandwich

This basic recipe for a creamed sponge cake can also be used to fill individual paper cake cases or tins for fairy cakes and butterfly cakes.

melted lard or oil for greasing 2 × 15cm/6in tins
110g/4oz butter
110g/4oz caster sugar
2 eggs, beaten
110g/4oz self-raising flour, sifted
water
2 tablespoons raspberry jam
caster sugar

1. Preheat the oven to 190°C/375°F/gas mark 5.
2. Lightly grease two 15cm/6in sandwich tins and line the base of each with a disc of greased greaseproof paper.
3. Cream the butter and sugar together in a mixing bowl until light and fluffy.
4. Beat the eggs gradually into the creamed mixture, beating well after each addition. Add 1 tablespoon of the flour if necessary to prevent the mixture from curdling.
5. Using a large metal spoon, fold in the remaining flour, adding enough water to bring the mixture to a dropping consistency. Divide the mixture between the prepared tins.
6. Bake in the centre of the oven for about 20 minutes or until the cakes are well risen, golden and feel spongy to the fingertips.
7. Remove the cakes from the oven and allow them to cool in the tins for a few minutes, then turn out on to a wire rack and leave to cool completely.
8. When the cakes are cold, sandwich them together with raspberry jam. Dust the top with caster sugar.

♦ ♦

Madeira Cake

melted lard or oil for greasing tin
170g/6oz unsalted butter
170g/6oz caster sugar
grated zest and juice of 1 lemon
a pinch of ground cinnamon
3 eggs, beaten
110g/4oz self-raising flour
55g/2oz ground almonds
milk (optional)

1. Grease an 18cm/7in cake tin and line the base with a disc of greased greaseproof paper.
2. Preheat the oven to 170°C/325°F/gas mark 3.
3. Cream the butter in a mixing bowl until soft. Beat in the sugar until light and fluffy. Add the lemon zest and cinnamon.
4. Add the eggs gradually, beating well after each addition. Add a little of the flour if necessary to prevent the mixture from curdling. Add the lemon juice.
5. Using a large metal spoon, fold in the remaining flour and the ground almonds.
6. Add enough milk to bring the mixture to a dropping consistency (it should drop rather than run off the spoon).
7. Spoon the mixture into the prepared tin and spread out evenly with a palette knife or spatula.
8. Bake in the centre of the oven for 1¼ hours or until the top springs back when pressed lightly with a fingertip. Remove the cake from the oven and allow to cool in the tin for 10 minutes, then gently ease it out on to a wire rack and leave to cool completely.

♦ ♦

Whisked Sponge

melted lard or oil for greasing tin
3 eggs
85g/3oz caster sugar
1½ tablespoons lukewarm water
85g/3oz plain flour, sifted
a pinch of salt

1. Preheat the oven to 180°C/350°F/gas mark 4. Grease a 20cm/8in moule-à-manqué cake tin and line the base with a disc of greased greaseproof paper. Dust lightly with sugar and then flour. Tap out the excess.
2. Place the eggs and sugar in a large heatproof bowl and fit it over (not in) a saucepan of gently simmering water. Whisk until the mixture is light, thick and fluffy. (If using an electric beater, no heat is required.)
3. Remove the bowl from the heat and continue whisking until slightly cooled. Add the water.
4. Sift the flour again with the salt and, using a large metal spoon, fold it into the mixture, being careful not to beat out any of the air. Turn the mixture into the prepared tin.
5. Bake in the centre of the oven for about 30 minutes or until the sides have shrunk away from the tin slightly and look crinkled, and the cake feels firm but spongy when pressed lightly with a fingertip and sounds 'creaky'.
6. Turn the cake out on to a wire rack and leave to cool completely.

◆◆◆◆◆◆◆◆◆◆◆◆◆◆◆◆◆◆◆◆◆◆

Swiss Roll

melted lard or oil for greasing tin
85g/3oz plain flour, sifted
a pinch of salt
3 eggs
85g/3oz caster sugar
1½ tablespoons lukewarm water
2–3 drops vanilla essence
caster sugar
3 tablespoons jam, warm but not hot.

1. Preheat the oven to 190°C/375°F/gas mark 5. Grease the base and sides of a Swiss roll tin. Line the base with a piece of greased greaseproof paper. Dust lightly with flour and then caster sugar. Tap out the excess.
2. Sift the flour with the salt.
3. Place the eggs and sugar in a large heatproof bowl and fit it over (not in) a saucepan of gently simmering water. Whisk until the mixture is light, thick and fluffy. (If using an electric beater, no heat is required.)
4. Using a large metal spoon, fold the water, vanilla essence and flour into the egg mixture and pour into the prepared tin.
5. Bake in the centre of the oven for 12–15 minutes until the sides have shrunk very slightly away from the tin, and no impression remains when the top is pressed lightly with a fingertip.
6. Lay a piece of greaseproof paper on the work surface and sprinkle it evenly with caster sugar. Using a knife, loosen the edges of the cake, then turn it out on to the sugared greaseproof paper. Remove the lining paper and trim the edges of the cake neatly.
7. While the cake is still warm, spread it with the jam.
8. Using the paper under the cake to help you, roll the cake up firmly from one end. Making a shallow cut across the width of the cake just where you begin to roll helps to get a good tight Swiss roll.
9. Dredge the cake with caster sugar. Transfer to a wire rack and leave to cool completely.

NOTE: If the Swiss roll is to be filled with cream, this cannot be done while it is hot. Roll the cake up, unfilled, and keep it wrapped in greaseproof paper until cool. Unroll carefully, spread with whipped cream, and roll up again.

◆◆◆◆◆◆◆◆◆◆◆◆◆◆◆◆◆◆◆◆◆◆

Sponge Fingers

MAKES 30
6 eggs
140g/5oz caster sugar
110g/4oz flour
30g/1oz arrowroot

1. Preheat the oven to 200°C/400°F/gas mark 6. Line 2 large baking sheets with silicone baking paper. Draw parallel lines 12.5cm/5in apart on the paper.
2. Separate 5 of the eggs. Beat the yolks with the whole egg and 110g/4oz of the sugar in a large bowl until the mixture is nearly white.
3. Whisk the egg whites until stiff and gradually whisk in the remaining sugar until stiff and shiny. Fold the egg whites into the yolk and sugar mixture, using a large metal spoon. Sift the flour with the arrowroot and fold in carefully.
4. Fit a 5mm/¼in plain pipe into a piping bag and fill the bag with the mixture. Pipe 12.5cm/5in fingers between the parallel lines on the baking paper. The fingers should be just touching.
5. Bake in the top of the oven for about 10 minutes or until the sponge has risen and is biscuit-coloured.
6. Remove the sponge fingers from the oven, invert on to a clean tea towel and immediately and carefully peel off the paper. Turn on to a wire rack and leave to cool completely.
7. Use either as a whole sheet of sponge fingers, as in Le Gascon (see page 87), or divide into individual fingers.

♦ ♦

Angel Cake

There are special Angel cake tins available on the market but any cake tin can be used. A springform tin with a funnel base is good. An Angel cake should be very light and airy, rather like a soufflé.

melted lard or oil for greasing tin
85g/3oz plain flour
170g/6oz caster sugar
6 egg whites
1 teaspoon cream of tartar
teaspoon vanilla essence

To decorate (optional)
1 egg white quantity American Frosting (see page 142)

1. Preheat the oven to 170°C/325°F/gas mark 3. Very lightly grease the base and sides of a 20cm/8in springform tin with a funnel base. Line the base with a disc of greased greaseproof paper.
2. Sift the flour 3 times (this is very important as the cake should be as light as air). Sift the sugar separately. Mix together the flour and 45g/1½oz sugar and sift well together.
3. Whisk the egg whites until very stiff, add the cream of tartar and 2 tablespoons of the remaining sugar and whisk again until stiff and shiny. Whisk in the remaining sugar gradually until the egg whites form stiff peaks.
4. Fold the flour and sugar mixture very

carefully into the egg whites, using a large metal spoon. Get rid of any large bubbles or pockets of flour, but do not overfold. Turn the mixture into the prepared tin.

5. Bake in the centre of the oven for 40 minutes or until the top springs back when pressed lightly with a fingertip.

6. Immediately turn the cake upside-down on to a wire rack. Leave to cool in the tin for 30 minutes, then remove very carefully from the tin. The cake will probably cling to the sides a little, so use a fork or knife to pull it away carefully. Leave to cool completely.

7. When the cake is cold, cover with American Frosting, if liked, or serve plain.

◆ ◆

Genoise Commune

melted lard or oil for greasing tin
4 eggs
125g/4½oz caster sugar
55g/2oz butter, melted and cooled
125g/4½oz plain flour

1. Preheat the oven to 190°C/375°F/gas mark 5. Grease a 20cm/8in moule-à-manqué or deep sandwich tin.

2. Break the eggs into a large heatproof bowl. Add the sugar. Fit the bowl over (not in) a saucepan of gently simmering water. Whisk until the mixture has doubled in bulk and will leave a ribbon trail on the surface when the whisk is lifted. Lift the bowl off the heat and continue to whisk until cool. (If using an electric beater, no heat is required.) Fold in the butter quickly; if you work slowly the cake will collapse.

3. Sift the flour over the mixture and fold it in thoroughly but gently, using a large metal spoon. Turn the mixture into the prepared tin.

4. Bake in the centre of the oven for 30–35 minutes until the top springs back when pressed lightly with a fingertip.

5. Remove the cake from the oven and allow to cool in the tin for a few minutes, then turn out on to a wire rack and leave to cool completely.

◆ ◆

Genoise Fine

oil for greasing tin
4 eggs
125g/4½oz caster sugar
100g/3½oz butter, melted and cooled
100g/3½oz plain flour

1. Preheat the oven to 190°C/375°F/gas mark 5. Grease a 20cm/8in moule-à-manqué or deep sandwich tin. Line the base with a disc of lightly greased greaseproof paper and dust lightly with caster sugar and then flour. Tap out the excess.

2. Break the eggs into a large heatproof bowl and add the sugar. Fit the bowl over (not in) a saucepan of gently simmering water and whisk until the mixture is light, fluffy and doubled in bulk. Remove from the heat and continue whisking until cool. (If using an

electric beater, no heat is required.) Fold in the butter quickly; if you work slowly the cake will collapse.

3. Sift the flour over the mixture and fold it in thoroughly but gently, using a large metal spoon. Turn the mixture into the prepared tin.

4. Bake in the centre of the oven for 30–35 minutes until the top springs back when pressed lightly with a fingertip.

5. Remove the cake from the oven and allow to cool in the tin for a few minutes, then turn out on to a wire rack and leave to cool completely.

NOTE: This is sometimes called a 'butter sponge'. However, this description is not culinarily correct, as a true sponge contains no fat.

◆ ◆

Rice Cake

melted lard or oil for greasing tin
110g/4oz butter
225g/8oz caster sugar
finely grated zest of ½ lemon
4 eggs
25g/8oz ground rice

1. Preheat the oven to 180°C/350°F/gas mark 4. Double-line an 18cm/7in cake tin with greased and floured greaseproof paper.
2. Cream the butter until soft in a mixing bowl. Beat in the sugar until light and fluffy. Add the lemon zest and mix well.
3. Separate the eggs. Add the yolks to the creamed mixture one at a time, beating hard

all the time.
4. Whisk the egg whites until fairly stiff but not dry. Take a spoonful of egg white and mix it into the creamed mixture. Stir in half the ground rice. Add half the remaining egg whites. Add the remaining ground rice, then the remaining egg white.
5. Turn the mixture into the prepared tin. Make a slight dip in the centre to counteract any tendency to rise in the middle.
6. Bake in the centre of the oven for 45 minutes or until slightly shrunken at the edges and firm to the touch.
7. Remove the cake from the oven and allow to cool in the tin for 5 minutes, then turn out on to a wire rack and leave to cool completely.

◆ ◆

Seed Cake

melted lard or oil for greasing tin
225g/8oz butter
170g/6oz caster sugar
3 eggs, beaten

225g/8oz self-raising flour
½ teaspoon ground mace
½ teaspoon freshly grated nutmeg
2 teaspoons caraway seeds
2 tablespoons brandy (optional)
1½ tablespoons water

1. Preheat the oven to 180°C/350°F/gas mark 4. Grease a 20cm/8in deep cake tin and line the base with a disc of greased greaseproof paper.

2. Cream the butter and sugar together in a mixing bowl until light and fluffy. Add the eggs gradually, beating well after each addition. Add a little of the flour if necessary, to prevent the mixture from curdling.

3. Sift together the remaining flour, mace and nutmeg and fold into the cake mixture, using a large metal spoon. Add the caraway seeds, brandy, if using, and water. Turn the mixture into the prepared cake tin and spread out evenly.

4. Bake in the centre of the oven for about 45 minutes or until the sides of the cake start to shrink away from the tin and the top springs back when pressed lightly with a fingertip.

5. Remove the cake from the oven and allow to cool in the tin for a few minutes, then turn out on to a wire rack and leave to cool completely.

◆ ◆

Battenburg Cake

This old-fashioned cake, named after Prince Henry of Battenburg, is really worth making. It is a thousand times removed from the shop-bought variety, which tends to be rather dry.

melted lard or oil for greasing tins
170g/6oz self-raising flour, sifted
1½ teaspoons baking powder
170g/6oz butter
170g/6oz caster sugar
3 large eggs, lightly beaten
3 tablespoons lukewarm water
red colouring
marzipan paste (see page 144)
apricot jam

1. Preheat the oven to 190°C/375°F/gas mark 5. Grease two 450g/1lb loaf tins and line the base of each with a piece of greased greaseproof paper.

2. Sift the flour with the baking powder.

Cream the butter in a mixing bowl, add the sugar and beat together until pale and creamy. Add the eggs gradually, beating well after each addition. Using a large metal spoon, fold in the remaining flour with the baking powder and add the water to achieve a softish dropping consistency.

3. Divide the mixture into two. Place one half in one of the prepared tins. Add 4-6 drops of red colouring to the other half until the mixture is very pink. Place in the other prepared tin.

4. Bake in the centre of the oven for about 35 minutes or until the sides of the cakes start to shrink away from the tins and the tops spring back when pressed lightly with a fingertip.

5. Remove the cakes from the oven and allow to cool in the tins for 5 minutes, then turn out on to a wire rack and leave to cool completely.

6. Meanwhile, make the marzipan paste.

7. When the cakes are cold, trim them and cut each into half lengthwise, to give 4 pieces

all the same size.

8. Spread each piece with apricot jam and
sandwich together in pairs, to give a
chequerboard effect. Spread the long sides
but not the ends of the cake with jam.

9. Roll out the marzipan quite thinly. Cut
to size and encase the cake with the
marzipan. Leave the ends uncovered. Trim
neatly.

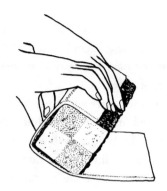

♦ ♦

Malt Loaf

This is particularly delicious served with
plenty of butter.

melted lard or oil to grease tins
450g/1lb plain flour
30g/1oz baking powder
55g/2oz soft dark brown sugar
170g/6oz dried dates, chopped
225g/8oz sultanas
55g/2oz butter
55g/2oz black treacle
110g/4oz malt extract
290ml/½ pint milk

1. Preheat the oven to 180°C/350°F/gas
mark 4. Grease two 675g/1½lb loaf tins and
line the base of each with a piece of greased
greaseproof paper.

2. Sift the flour with the baking powder into
a large mixing bowl. Add the sugar, dates
and sultanas.

3. Melt the butter, add the treacle and malt
extract and heat very gently until the
mixture is runny. Add the milk and mix
well.

4. Make a well in the flour mixture. Add the
liquid ingredients and mix very well to get a
smooth soft dough. Spoon into the prepared
tins.

5. Bake in the centre of the oven for 1–1½
hours or until a sharp knife or skewer
inserted into the centre of the loaves comes
out clean.

6. Remove the loaves from the oven and
allow to cool in the tins for 10 minutes, then
turn on to a wire rack and leave to cool
completely.

♦ ♦

Yorkshire Parkin

Parkin is best stored for about a week before eating. It can be stored in a tin or wrapped in kitchen foil. Serve it cut into squares or thick slices. It is traditionally served on November 5th.

melted lard or oil for greasing tin
225g/8oz plain flour
2 teaspoons baking powder
2 teaspoons ground ginger
55g/2oz butter
55g/2oz lard
225g/8oz medium oatmeal
110g/4oz caster sugar
170g/6oz golden syrup
170g/6oz black treacle
4 tablespoons milk

1. Preheat the oven to 180°C/350°F/gas mark 4. Grease a shallow 25 × 20cm/ 10 × 8in tin and line the base with a piece of greased greaseproof paper.
2. Sift the flour, baking powder and ginger together into a large mixing bowl. Cut the butter and lard into pieces and rub into the flour until the mixture resembles fine breadcrumbs. Stir in the oatmeal and sugar. Make a well in the centre of the mixture.
3. Put the syrup and treacle into a saucepan and warm gently. Pour into the well. Add the milk and mix well until all the flour is incorporated. Turn the mixture into the prepared tin.
4. Bake in the centre of the oven for about 45 minutes or until the sides of the cake have shrunk away from the tin.
5. Turn out on to a wire rack and leave to cool completely.

◆ ◆

Rock Buns

These delicious little cakes suffer from having a name which makes them sound unappetizing. They are supposed to look like little rocks, not taste like them! Once made they should be eaten quickly or frozen as they go stale quickly.

MAKES 10
225g/8oz self-raising flour
a pinch of salt
110g/4oz butter
85g/3oz caster sugar
55g/2oz sultanas
55g/2oz raisins
30g/1oz chopped mixed peel

2 eggs, beaten
milk

1. Preheat the oven to 190°C/375°F/gas mark 5. Grease a baking sheet.
2. Sift the flour with the salt into a mixing bowl. Cut the butter into pieces and rub in until the mixture resembles fine breadcrumbs. Add the sugar and fruit and mix well. Stir in the eggs and enough milk to bind. The mixture should be quite stiff.
3. Using 2 forks, put heaps of the mixture, about the size of a small egg, on to a baking sheet, 5cm/2in apart to allow for spreading.
4. Bake for 15–20 minutes until pale brown. Transfer the buns on to a wire rack and leave to cool completely.

♦♦♦♦♦♦♦♦♦♦♦♦♦♦♦♦♦♦♦♦♦♦♦

Gâteau Nougatine

This classic gâteau will take about a day to complete.

For the cake
melted lard or oil for greasing tin
110g/4oz hazelnuts
4 eggs
1 egg white
120g/4½oz caster sugar
55g/2oz butter, softened
100g/3½oz plain flour, sifted

For the royal icing
1 small egg white
170g/6oz icing sugar
a squeeze of lemon juice

For the nougat
45g/1½oz almonds, finely chopped
85g/3oz caster sugar
2 teaspoons powdered glucose or a pinch of
    cream of tartar

For the crème au beurre mousseline
85g/3oz lump or granulated sugar
3 tablespoons water
2 egg yolks
110–140g/4–5oz unsalted butter

For the chocolate fondant icing
225g/8oz loaf sugar
½ teaspoon liquid glucose or a pinch of cream of
    tartar
115ml/4fl oz water

30g/1oz unsweetened plain chocolate, chopped
1 drop of vanilla essence

1. Preheat the oven to 180°C/350°F/gas mark 4.
2. Grease a 20cm/8in moule-à-manqué tin and line with a disc of greased greaseproof paper. Dust first with caster sugar and then with flour. Tap out the excess.
3. Spread the hazelnuts out on a baking sheet and brown in the oven for 10–15 minutes. Remove the skins and allow to cool, then grind finely.
4. Make the cake: separate the eggs. Beat the yolks and 1 white with all but 1 tablespoon of the sugar until pale and creamy.
5. Whisk the remaining egg whites until stiff. Whisk in the reserved sugar until stiff and shiny.
6. Quickly add the butter to the egg yolk mixture. Mix the flour with the ground hazelnuts. Fold the egg whites into the yolk mixture, using a large metal spoon, and then fold in the flour and nuts. Pile into the prepared tin.
7. Bake in the centre of the oven for 40–50 minutes or until the sides have shrunk away from the tin slightly and the top springs back when pressed lightly with a fingertip. Turn out on to a wire rack and leave to cool completely.
8. Make the royal icing: whisk the egg white until frothy. Beat in the icing sugar, with the lemon juice, until very smooth, white and stiff. Cover with a damp cloth until ready for use.

9. Oil a baking sheet.

10. Make the nougat: bake the almonds in the oven until pale brown. Keep warm. Put the sugar and glucose or cream of tartar into a heavy saucepan and place over a medium heat until melted and golden. Add the almonds and cook for 1 further minute.

11. Pour the mixture on to the oiled baking sheet. Turn it over with an oiled palette knife, using a half-mixing, half-kneading movement. While still warm and pliable, roll the nougat out as thinly as possible, using an oiled lemon.

12. Make the crème au beurre mousseline: dissolve the sugar in the water in a heavy saucepan. Boil until a little syrup forms short, sticky threads when pulled between a wet finger and thumb. Whisk the egg yolks and pour on the sugar syrup in a steady stream, whisking constantly. Continue whisking until thick and mousse-like. Cream the butter in a bowl until soft, then add the mousse and combine thoroughly.

13. Make the chocolate fondant icing: dissolve the sugar with the glucose or cream of tartar in the water in a saucepan over a low heat without boiling. Cover and bring to the boil. Boil to the soft ball stage (110–115°C/230–240°F). Meanwhile, scrub a stainless steel or heat-resistant work surface and sprinkle with water. Stop the sugar syrup from cooking further by dipping the bottom of the pan into a bowl of very cold water. Cool slightly.

14. Put the chocolate into a heatproof bowl and melt over a saucepan of simmering water. Pour the sugar syrup slowly on to the moistened stainless steel top. Using a wet palette knife, fold the outsides of the mixture into the centre. When opaque but still fairly soft, add the melted chocolate and vanilla essence and continue to turn with a spatula until the fondant becomes fairly stiff. Put into a heatproof bowl and set over (not in) a saucepan of simmering water to soften.

15. To assemble: when the cake is cold, split horizontally into 3 layers. Crush the nougat with a rolling pin and mix half of it with half the crème au beurre mousseline. Sandwich the cake together with the mixture. Pour the melted chocolate fondant icing over the top of the cake. Spread the remaining crème au beurre mousseline around the sides and press on the remaining crushed nougat.

16. When the chocolate has set, fill a piping bag fitted with a writing nozzle with the royal icing and pipe the word 'nougatine' across the top.

♦ ♦

Dobez Torte

This is a Hungarian cake in 5 layers. The mixture will not deteriorate if lack of baking sheets or space in the oven means that all the layers cannot be baked at the same time.

For the cake
4 eggs
170g/6oz caster sugar
140g/5oz plain flour
a pinch of salt

For the butter cream
85g/3oz granulated sugar
4–5 tablespoons water
3 egg yolks
225g/8oz unsalted butter
coffee essence
55g/2oz hazelnuts, skinned, toasted and ground

To decorate
5 whole hazelnuts, browned and skinned
sugar
chopped almonds or ground hazelnuts

1. Preheat the oven to 190°C/375°F/gas mark 5. Grease and flour 5 baking sheets and use a flan ring or saucepan lid to mark a 20cm/8in circle on each sheet. Alternatively, use silicone baking paper.
2. Make the cake: whisk the eggs in a heatproof bowl and gradually whisk in the sugar. Fit the bowl over (not in) a saucepan of gently simmering water and whisk until the mixture is thick and mousse-like. Remove from the heat and continue whisking until cool. Sift the flour with the salt and fold into the egg mixture, using a large metal spoon. Divide the mixture between the prepared baking sheets and spread quickly into circles as marked.

3. Bake in the centre of the oven for 8 minutes or until the cake layers spring back when pressed lightly with a fingertip. Trim the edges neatly and leave to cool on a wire rack.
4. Make the butter cream: put the sugar and water into a saucepan and stir over a low heat until the sugar has dissolved completely. When clear, bring to the boil and boil rapidly until a little syrup forms short, sticky threads when pulled between a wet finger and thumb. Allow to cool slightly for about 1 minute.
5. Whisk the egg yolks in a bowl and pour on the syrup in a slow, steady stream, whisking constantly. Continue whisking until the mixture is thick and mousse-like. Cream the butter in a bowl until soft, then beat in the egg and sugar mixture.
6. Flavour 2 tablespoons of the butter cream with coffee essence to taste and reserve for decoration. Mix the ground hazelnuts and a little coffee essence into the remaining butter cream.
7. Place one layer of cake on a wire rack set over an oiled baking sheet. Melt the sugar for the caramel in a little water in a saucepan, then boil fiercely until a good caramel colour. Pour immediately over the layer of cake, covering it completely.
8. Allow to harden slightly, then mark into 6 portions with an oiled knife, cutting through the setting caramel but not through the cake. Trim the edges of excess caramel.
9. Sandwich the cake layers together with coffee and hazelnut butter cream and spread it thinly around the sides. Press on the nuts.
10. Fill a piping bag fitted with a large fluted nozzle with the reserved coffee butter cream and pipe a rosette on top of each portion of cake. Decorate each rosette with a whole hazelnut.

◆ ◆

Choux à la Crème

The choux pastry can be made in advance, spooned on to the baking sheet and frozen before it is baked. The choux buns can then be baked from frozen. Once the Choux à la Crème have been assembled, they will last for about 1½ hours before they go soggy.

The choux pastry can also be piped into fingers to make eclairs. Fill with sweetened whipped cream and coat with chocolate or coffee glacé icing.

MAKES 8–10
55g/2oz butter
150ml/5fl oz water
70g/2½oz plain flour, well sifted
a pinch of salt
2 eggs, beaten

For the filling
425ml/¾ pint double cream
icing sugar, sifted
fresh fruit, such as strawberries, raspberries, peaches, apricots, washed and sliced as necessary

1. Preheat the oven to 200°C/400°F/gas mark 6.
2. Cut the butter into cubes and put into a saucepan with the water. Bring slowly to the boil so that by the time the water boils, the butter is completely melted.
3. Immediately the mixture is boiling really fast, tip in all the flour with the salt and remove the pan from the heat.
4. Working as fast as you can, beat the mixture hard with a wooden spoon: it will soon become thick and smooth and leave the sides of the pan. Do not overbeat at this stage. Leave to cool.
5. When the mixture is cool, beat in the eggs gradually until it is soft, shiny and smooth. If the eggs are large, it may not be necessary to add all of them. The mixture should be of a dropping consistency.
6. Place spoonfuls of the mixture 5cm/2in apart on a baking sheet. Bake in the top of the oven for about 30 minutes or until the buns are brown and crisp.
7. Remove from the oven and make a hole in the side of each bun to let the steam escape. Return to the oven for 5 minutes to dry the insides out. Transfer to a wire rack and leave to cool completely.
8. Meanwhile, whip the cream until fairly stiff and sweeten with 1–2 tablespoons icing sugar.
9. Split the buns in half and place a spoonful of the whipped cream and some fruit inside. Dust the tops with sifted icing sugar.

2   FRUIT CAKES

The addition of dried fruit such as sultanas, raisins, dates and apricots makes a cake moist and helps with its keeping quality. Any cake that contains a lot of dried fruit generally needs to be baked at a lower oven temperature and for a longer time than other cakes, because of the fruit's high sugar content. The tins should have several layers of newspapers wrapped round them (see page 30). It is very important to keep an eye on large fruit cakes during baking, covering with greaseproof paper and turning down the oven temperature if necessary, to prevent over-browning on top while the cake cooks through.

Cakes made with fresh fruit are delicious, and often make good puddings: do not be tempted to add too much fruit to the mixture, as it produces a lot of liquid during baking, which could make the cake soggy and prevent it from rising.

Cakes with dried and glacé fruit

❖ ❖

Light Fruit Cake

melted lard or oil for greasing tin
170g/6oz butter
170g/6oz caster sugar
3 eggs, beaten
340g/12oz self-raising flour
½ teaspoon ground mixed spice
½ teaspoon ground cinnamon
150ml/5fl oz milk
225g/8oz mixed dried fruit, such as sultanas, raisins, currants, chopped apricots, chopped prunes

1. Preheat the oven to 180°C/350°F/gas mark 4. Grease a 20cm/8in deep cake tin.
2. Cream the butter and sugar together in a large mixing bowl until light and fluffy. Add the eggs gradually, beating well after each addition.
3. Sift together the flour and spices and fold into the creamed mixture, using a large metal spoon. Add the milk and fruit and mix well. Turn into the prepared tin.
4. Bake in the centre of the oven for 1¼–1½ hours or until a sharp knife or skewer inserted into the centre of the cake comes out clean.
5. Remove the cake from the oven and allow to cool completely in the tin before turning out.

♦ ♦

Dundee Cake

melted lard or oil for greasing tin
225g/8oz butter
225g/8oz caster sugar
grated zest of 1 lemon
5 eggs (size 4), beaten
225g/8oz plain flour, sifted
340g/12oz sultanas
340g/12oz currants
170g/6oz chopped mixed peel
110g/4oz glacé cherries
30g/1oz blanched almonds, chopped
55g/2oz split blanched almonds

1. Preheat the oven to 150°C/300°F/gas mark 2. Grease a 20cm/8in deep cake tin. Line the base and sides with greased greaseproof paper (see page 30).

2. Cream the butter and sugar together in a large mixing bowl until light and fluffy. Add the lemon zest.

3. Add the eggs gradually, beating well after each addition. Add a little of the flour if necessary to prevent the mixture from curdling.

4. Fold in the flour and the dried fruit, peel, cherries and chopped almonds, using a large metal spoon. Mix together carefully. Turn into the prepared tin and spread out evenly.

5. Arrange the split almonds in concentric circles on the top of the cake.

6. Bake in the centre of the oven for 3–3½ hours or until a sharp knife or skewer inserted into the centre comes out clean.

7. Remove the cake from the oven and allow to cool completely in the tin before turning out.

♦ ♦

Cherry Cake

melted lard or oil for greasing tin
170g/6oz butter
170g/6 oz caster sugar
3 eggs, beaten
140g/5oz self-raising flour
55g/2oz plain flour
225g/8oz glacé cherries, halved, washed and
*   dried*
85g/3oz ground almonds

1. Preheat the oven to 180°C/350°F/gas mark 4. Grease an 18cm/7in deep cake tin and line the base with a disc of greased greaseproof paper.

2. Cream the butter and sugar together in a mixing bowl until light and fluffy. Add the eggs slowly, beating well after each addition.

3. Sift together the flours and add the cherries and ground almonds. Fold into the creamed mixture, using a large metal spoon. Turn into the prepared tin and make a small dip in the centre to counteract any tendency to rise in the middle.

4. Bake in the centre of the oven for 1–1½ hours or until a sharp knife or skewer inserted into the centre comes out clean.

5. Remove the cake from the oven and allow to cool in the tin for 20 minutes, then turn out on to a wire rack and leave to cool completely.

Bitter-sweet Fruit Cake

melted lard or oil for greasing tin
225g/8oz raisins
225g/8oz sultanas
finely grated zest and juice of 1 orange
110g/4oz butter
110g/4oz caster sugar
1½ tablespoons honey
140g/5oz plain chocolate, chopped
2 eggs, beaten
110g/4oz plain wholemeal flour
1 teaspoon ground mixed spice
55g/2oz pinenuts

1. Preheat the oven to 170°C/325°F/gas mark 3. Grease a 15cm/6in deep cake tin and line the base and sides with greased greaseproof paper (see page 30).
2. Put the dried fruit, orange zest and juice, butter, sugar, honey and chocolate into a large saucepan. Heat gently until the chocolate and butter have melted, stirring occasionally. Remove from the heat and allow to cool.
3. Add the eggs and mix thoroughly. Stir in the flour, mixed spice and pinenuts. Turn the mixture into the prepared tin.
4. Bake in the centre of the oven for 40 minutes, then reduce the temperature to 150°C/300°F/gas mark 2 and bake for 50 further minutes or until a sharp knife or skewer inserted into the centre of the cake comes out clean.
5. Remove the cake from the oven and allow to cool completely in the tin before turning out.

Upside-down Toffee Gingerbread

This can be served as a cake or a very indulgent winter pudding with Greek yoghurt to accompany.

For the toffee topping
55g/2oz unsalted butter
85g/3oz soft light brown sugar
½ teaspoon ground ginger
6 dried figs, roughly chopped
8 dried pears
75g/2½oz macadamia nuts

For the gingerbread
melted lard or oil for greasing tin
110g/4oz butter
110g/4oz soft light brown sugar
110g/4oz black treacle
225g/8oz plain flour
2 teaspoons ground ginger
2 eggs, beaten

85ml/3fl oz milk
1 teaspoon bicarbonate of soda
2 tablespoons stem ginger, diced

1. Preheat the oven to 180°C/350°F/gas mark 4. Grease a 20cm/8in moule-à-manqué or round cake tin.
2. Make the toffee topping: melt the butter and stir in the sugar and ginger. Pour into the prepared tin.
3. Arrange the dried fruit and nuts on the toffee.
4. Make the gingerbread: melt the butter, sugar and treacle together in a saucepan over a low heat. Do not let the mixture boil. Remove from the heat and allow to cool.
5. Sift the flour with the ground ginger into a large mixing bowl and make a well in the centre. Pour in the eggs and melted mixture. Using a wooden spoon, gradually draw in the flour and mix to a smooth batter.
6. Warm the milk to blood heat, add the bicarbonate of soda and pour into the batter with the stem ginger. Mix well. Pour carefully on to the fruit and nuts in the prepared tin.
7. Bake in the centre of the oven for about 45 minutes or until a sharp knife or skewer inserted into the centre of the cake comes out clean.
8. While the cake is still warm, turn it upside-down on to a wire rack and leave to cool completely.

◆ ◆

Fruit Tea Loaf

Soaking the fruit in tea prior to cooking gives this fatless cake a wonderfully moist texture and an unusual, delicious taste of its own. The results are best if you soak the fruit overnight or for about 12 hours.

110g/4oz sultanas
110g/4oz raisins
55g/2oz currants
55g/2oz chopped mixed peel
110g/4oz soft dark brown sugar
290ml/½ pint cold tea (preferably Indian)
225g/8oz self-raising flour
1 egg, beaten

1. Soak the dried fruit, peel and sugar in the cold tea overnight.
2. Preheat the oven to 170°C/325°F/gas mark 3. Grease a 900g/2lb loaf tin and line the base with a piece of greased greaseproof paper.
3. Stir the flour into the soaked fruit mixture and mix in the egg thoroughly. Turn into the prepared tin. Bake in the centre of the oven for 1¼ hours or until a sharp knife or skewer inserted into the centre of the loaf comes out clean.
4. Remove the cake from the oven and allow to cool in the tin for 10 minutes, then turn on to a wire rack and leave to cool completely.

◆ ◆

Wensleydale Fruit Cake

melted lard or oil for greasing tin
225g/8oz butter
225g/8oz soft light brown sugar
5 eggs, beaten
285g/10oz plain flour
½ teaspoon ground cinnamon
110g/4oz currants
110g/4oz sultanas
110g/4oz raisins
110g/4oz dried apples, chopped
170g/6oz Wensleydale cheese, thinly sliced

1. Preheat the oven to 170°C/325°F/gas
mark 3. Grease a 20cm/8in deep cake tin
and line the base and sides with greased
greaseproof paper (see page 30).
2. Cream the butter in a large mixing bowl,
add the sugar and beat until light and
creamy. Add the eggs gradually, beating well
after each addition. Add a little of the flour if
necessary to prevent the mixture from
curdling.
3. Sift together the flour and cinnamon and
add to the creamed mixture with the fruit.
Mix well.
4. Put half the mixture into the prepared tin
and smooth flat. Cover with the slices of
Wensleydale cheese and put the remaining
cake mixture on top. Smooth flat.
5. Bake in the centre of the oven for 2–2½
hours or until a sharp knife or skewer
inserted into the centre of the cake comes
out clean.
6. Remove the cake from the oven and
allow to cool completely in the tin before
turning out.

NOTE: If the top starts to get too dark
during baking, cover with a piece of
greaseproof paper or kitchen foil. The cake
will keep for a week or so in a tin or can be
frozen.

◆ ◆ ◆ ◆ ◆ ◆ ◆ ◆ ◆ ◆ ◆ ◆ ◆ ◆ ◆ ◆ ◆ ◆ ◆ ◆

Simnel Cake

A festive Easter cake: the 11 balls of
marzipan are said to represent the apostles
(without Judas). Sometimes they are shaped
like eggs, the symbol of spring and rebirth.

melted lard or oil for greasing tin
a large pinch each of salt and baking powder
225g/8oz plain flour
55g/2oz rice flour
110g/4oz glacé cherries
225g/8oz butter
225g/8oz caster sugar
grated zest of 1 lemon
4 eggs
225g/8oz sultanas
110g/4oz currants
30g/1oz chopped mixed peel
340g/12 oz marzipan (see page 144)
beaten egg
110g/4oz glacé icing (see page 139)

1. Preheat the oven to 180°C/350°F/gas
mark 4. Double-line the base and sides of a
20cm/8in cake tin with greased and floured
greaseproof paper. Wrap the outside of the
cake tin with a double thickness of

newspaper to insulate the cake from direct heat. Secure with string (see page 30).

2. Sift together the salt, baking powder and flours. Cut the cherries in half.

3. Cream the butter in a mixing bowl until soft. Add the sugar and beat until light and fluffy. Add the lemon zest and mix well.

4. Separate the eggs. Beat the egg yolks into the creamed mixture. Whisk the whites until stiff.

5. Using a large metal spoon, fold three-quarters of the flour into the mixture. Fold in the egg whites gradually, alternating with the remaining flour and the cherries, dried fruit and peel.

6. Put half the mixture into the prepared tin.

7. Take just over three-quarters of the marzipan paste. Roll it to a smooth 20cm/8in diameter round. Place it in the cake tin. Cover with the remaining mixture.

8. Make a small dip in the centre of the cake

to counteract any tendency to rise in the middle.

9. Bake for 2 hours in the centre of the oven, then reduce the oven temperature to 150°C/300°F/gas mark 2. Bake for 30 further minutes or until a sharp knife or skewer inserted into the centre of the cake comes out clean. Remove from the oven and allow to cool completely in the tin before turning out.

10. Roll the remaining marzipan to a circle the same size as the top of the cake. Cut a piece from the centre about 12.5cm/5in in diameter and shape into 11 small even balls.

11. Heat the grill. Lay the ring of marzipan on top of the cake and brush with beaten egg. Arrange the marzipan balls on top of the ring and brush again with beaten egg. Grill until golden-brown.

12. When the cake is cold, pour a little glacé icing into the centre of the marzipan ring. Tie a ribbon around the sides of the cake.

◆ ◆

Mincemeat Cake

This very moist cake is good for using up leftover mincemeat after Christmas.

melted lard or oil for greasing tin
225g/8oz sultanas
30g/1oz chopped mixed peel
85ml/3fl oz warm tea, preferably Indian
170g/6oz butter
170g/6oz demerara sugar
2 eggs
225g/8oz self-raising flour
2 teaspoons ground mixed spice
225g/8oz mincemeat
2 tablespoons marmalade

1. Soak the sultanas and mixed peel in the tea for 2 hours.

2. Preheat the oven to 150°C/300°F/gas mark 2. Grease an 18cm/7in cake tin and line the base and sides with greased greaseproof paper.

3. Cream the butter and sugar together in a large mixing bowl until light and fluffy. Add the eggs gradually, beating well after each addition.

4. Sift the flour with the mixed spice and fold into the creamed mixture, using a large metal spoon.

5. Add the soaked sultanas, peel, tea, mincemeat and marmalade. Stir well

together and turn into the prepared tin.
6. Bake in the centre of the oven for 2¼–2½
hours or until a sharp knife or skewer
inserted into the centre of the cake comes
out clean.
7. Remove the cake from the oven and
allow to cool completely in the tin before
turning out.

◆ ◆

Christmas Cake

melted lard or oil for greasing tin
110g/4oz glacé cherries
55g/2oz chopped mixed peel
450g/1lb raisins
285g/10oz sultanas
110g/4oz currants
225g/8oz butter
225g/8oz soft light brown sugar
5 eggs, beaten
285g/10oz plain flour, sifted
2 teaspoons ground mixed spice
grated zest of 1 lemon
2 tablespoons black treacle
2 wineglasses (200ml/7fl oz) beer or sherry
110g/4oz ground almonds

1. Preheat the oven to 170°C/325°F/gas
mark 3. Prepare a 22cm/9in round cake tin
or a 20cm/8in square cake tin (see page 26).
2. Cut up the cherries and mix with the
remaining fruit.
3. Cream the butter in a large mixing bowl
until soft. Add the sugar and beat together
until light and fluffy.
4. Add the eggs gradually, beating well after
each addition. Add 1 teaspoon of the flour if
necessary to prevent the mixture from
curdling.
5. Fold in the flour, mixed spice, lemon zest,
treacle and beer or sherry, using a large
metal spoon.
6. Stir in the ground almonds and the fruit.
7. Turn the mixture into the prepared tin
and make a deep hollow in the centre to
counteract any tendency to rise in the
middle.
8. Bake in the centre of the oven for 2½
hours or until a sharp knife or skewer
inserted into the centre of the cake comes
out clean.
9. Remove the cake from the oven and
allow it to cool completely in the tin before
turning out.

NOTE: This cake must now be covered with
marzipan (see page 144) before being
generously iced with royal icing (see page
147). If your family does not like icing, cover
the top with marzipan, rough it lightly with
a fork and toast it under the grill until
golden-brown.

Old-fashioned Boiled Christmas Cake

This cake is not, as the name suggests, boiled instead of baked. The fruit is boiled in water and orange juice and allowed to stand for 3 days before use, which gives it a wonderful plumpness. Instead of being decorated with marzipan and icing, the cake is finished with a glazed fruit and nut topping, and tied with a pretty ribbon.

melted lard or oil for greasing tin
225g/8oz butter, chopped
225g/8oz sultanas
225g/8oz raisins
110g/4oz currants
170g/6oz dried apricots, chopped
55g/2oz dried apples, chopped
110g/4oz dried dates, chopped
110g/4oz dried peaches, chopped
110g/4oz dried pears, chopped
55g/2oz chopped mixed peel
55g/2oz glacé cherries, halved
225g/8oz soft dark brown sugar
grated zest and juice of 1 lemon
grated zest and juice of 1 orange
110ml/4fl oz water
110ml/4fl oz orange juice
110ml/4fl oz brandy
½ teaspoon freshly grated nutmeg
1 teaspoon ground cinnamon
1 teaspoon ground allspice
½ teaspoon ground ginger
¼ teaspoon ground cardamom
1 tablespoon black treacle
5 eggs, beaten
310g/11oz plain flour
1 teaspoon baking powder

For the fruit and nut topping
340g/12oz apricot jam
340g/12oz mixed dried and glacé fruit and nuts,
*   such as pecans, brazils, almonds, apricots, red*
*   and green glacé cherries, prunes, peaches,*
*   pears*

1. Put the butter into a large saucepan over a low heat, add the dried fruit, peel, cherries, butter, sugar, lemon and orange zest and juice, water and the 110ml/4fl oz orange juice. Bring slowly up to the boil. Stir with a wooden spoon, cover with a lid, and simmer slowly for 10 minutes.

2. Remove from the heat and allow to cool slightly. Add the brandy and spices, and transfer to a large bowl. When the mixture is completely cold, cover and leave in a cool place (not the refrigerator) for 3 days, stirring daily.

3. Preheat the oven to 170°C/325°F/gas mark 3. Grease a 25cm/10in deep cake tin and double-line the base and sides with greased greaseproof paper (see page 30).

4. Stir the treacle into the boiled fruit mixture and beat in the eggs. Sift the flour with the baking powder and stir into the cake mixture, which will be slightly sloppy. Pour into the prepared tin.

5. Bake in the bottom of the oven for 4–4½ hours or until a sharp knife or skewer inserted into the centre of the cake comes out clean. If the cake top becomes very dark, cover it with a double layer of damp greaseproof paper and reduce the oven temperature to 150°C/300°F/gas mark 2.

6. Remove the cake from the oven and allow to cool completely in the tin before turning out.

7. When the cake is cold, wrap carefully in kitchen foil until ready to decorate. The cake will mature well for 2–3 months.

8. To decorate the cake: put the apricot jam into a saucepan with 1 tablespoon water. Heat until boiling, then push through a sieve. Allow to cool slightly, then brush the top of the cake with the apricot glaze. Arrange the fruit and nuts all over the top of the cake, then brush carefully with apricot glaze.

NOTE: The cake does tend to get quite dark and hard on the top but this softens after the glaze has been on for an hour or so.

The glaze will remain shiny on the cake for a few days but after a week it will begin to lose its gloss, so it is better not to decorate the cake too early.

◆ ◆

Rich Fruit Cake

This is ideal to use for a wedding or other celebration cake. The table opposite will give you the ingredient qualities to use for different-sized cakes. Rich Fruit Cake is best if allowed to mature for 2–3 months but can be used sooner.

Method
1. Preheat the oven to 150°C/300°F/gas mark 2. Grease and line the base and sides of the cake tin with a double layer of greaseproof paper and protect the sides by tying a couple of layers of newspaper around the outside of the tin (see page 30).
2. Cut the cherries in half and mix with the mixed peel, raisins, sultanas, currants, grated lemon zest and blanched chopped almonds.
3. Cream the butter until soft, add the sugar and beat well until light and fluffy. Beat the eggs and add gradually, beating well between each addition. If the mixture looks as if it might curdle, add a spoonful of flour.

4. Sift together the flour and mixed spice and fold into the mixture with the treacle.
5. Fold in the fruit and nut mixture. The brandy can be added now or it can be poured over the cake once it is baked.
6. Put the mixture into the prepared tin and place in the centre of the oven. Bake for the required time (see table). If it is a large cake (i.e. larger than 25cm/10in square or 28cm/11in round) you should turn the oven temperature down to 140°C/275°F/gas mark 1 after three-quarters of the baking time. If the top is getting too dark, cover with a piece of damp greaseproof paper. Test by inserting a sharp knife or skewer into the centre. If it comes out clean, the cake is ready.
7. Remove from the oven and allow to cool completely in the tin. When the cake is cold, remove from the tin but keep it in its greaseproof paper. Make a few holes in the top of the cake and pour over the brandy, if using or not already added. Wrap the cake well in kitchen foil and store in a cool, dry place.

Square cake sizes		15cm/6in	18cm/7in	20cm/8in	22cm/9in	25cm/10in	28cm/11in	30cm/12in
Round cake sizes	15cm/6in	18cm/7in	20cm/8in	22cm/9in	25cm/10in	28cm/11in	30cm/12in	
glacé cherries	45g/1½oz	70g/2½oz	85g/3oz	110g/4oz	140g/5oz	225g/8oz	285g/10oz	340g/12oz
chopped mixed peel	30g/1oz	55g/2oz	55g/2oz	85g/3oz	110g/4oz	140g/5oz	200g/7oz	250g/9oz
raisins	140g/5oz	225g/8oz	340g/12oz	450g/1lb	620g/1lb 6oz	790g/1lb 12oz	1.12kg/2lb 8oz	1.35kg/3lb
sultanas	55g/2oz	85g/3oz	110g/4oz	200g/7oz	225g/8oz	370g/13oz	425g/15oz	500g/1lb 2oz
currants	55g/2oz	85g/3oz	110g/4oz	200g/7oz	225g/8oz	370g/13oz	425g/15oz	500g/1lb 2oz
grated lemon zest	¼ lemon	½ lemon	1 lemon	1 lemon	1 lemon	1½ lemons	1½ lemons	2 lemons
blanched almonds – chopped	30g/1oz	55g/2oz	55g/2oz	85g/3oz	110g/4oz	140g/5oz	200g/7oz	250g/9oz
butter	85g/3oz	140g/5oz	170g/6oz	285g/10oz	340g/12oz	500g/1lb 2oz	590g/1lb 5oz	790g/1lb 12oz
soft brown sugar	85g/3oz	140g/5oz	170g/6oz	285g/10oz	340g/12oz	500g/1lb 2oz	590g/1lb 5oz	790g/1lb 12oz
eggs	2	2½	3	5	6	9	11	14
plain flour	110g/4oz	170g/6oz	225g/8oz	340g/12oz	450g/1lb	560g/1¼lb	675g/1½lb	790g/1lb 12oz
ground mixed spice	¼ teasp	½ teasp	¾ teasp	1 teasp	1½ teasp	2 teasp	2½ teasp	2¾ teasp
black treacle	½ tblsp	½ tblsp	1 tblsp	1½ tblsp	2 tblsp	2½ tblsp	3 tblsp	3½ tblsp
brandy (can be added after cooking)	2 tblsp	3 tblsp	4 tblsp	4½ tblsp	5 tblsp	5½ tblsp	6 tblsp	6½ tblsp
cooking time	2 hours	2½ hours	2¾ hours	3¼ hours	3½–4 hours	4–4½ hours	5–5½ hours	6–6½ hours

Wedding Cakes

It is very important to leave yourself enough time to make and decorate a wedding cake. The cakes should be made, if possible, at least 3 months before the wedding. They should then be stored in a cool, dry place, well wrapped. One month before the wedding, cover the cakes with marzipan (see page 144) and leave to dry, uncovered, in a cool, dry place for 1 week. Base-ice the cakes 3 weeks before the wedding, to ensure that they are strong enough to hold the weight of the other cakes. The decoration can be done 1 week before the wedding, with any 'run-out' work (see page 152) being done before then. Cover the decorated cake with soft tissue paper to prevent dust from collecting on it.

When you are planning to make a wedding cake, choose the sizes of the tiers carefully so that they are in proportion. For example, a three-tier cake of 30cm/12in, 22cm/9in and 15cm/6in works well, as does a two-tier cake of 30cm/12in and 20cm/8in. The bottom tier should be slightly deeper than the upper tiers.

The following table gives ingredients and baking times for various tin sizes, using the recipe for Old-fashioned Boiled Christmas Cake (see page 51). This works very well as a wedding cake but care must be taken when baking to avoid burning the top. The tins should be greased and double-lined with greaseproof paper, and the sides protected by newspaper tied around the outside of the tins, as described on page 30. For the larger cakes preheat the oven to 150°C/300°F/gas mark 2 and lower the temperature if the cake is getting too dark. In addition put a piece of damp greaseproof paper over the top.

The baking times given are not definitive but intended as a guide. Every oven varies, and cakes that are to be baked for a long time must be tested carefully by inserting a sharp knife into the centre. If it comes out clean, the cake is ready. Remove the cake from the oven and allow to cool completely in the tin before turning out. Store wrapped in greaseproof paper and kitchen foil.

Square cake sizes		15cm/6in	18cm/7in	20cm/8in	22cm/9in	25cm/10in	28cm/11in	30cm/12in
Round cake sizes	15cm/6in	18cm/7in	20cm/8in	22cm/9in	25cm/10in	28cm/11in	30cm/12in	
sultanas	85g/3oz	110g/4oz	140g/5oz	170g/6oz	225g/8oz	340g/12oz	500g/1lb 2oz	750g/1lb 11oz
raisins	85g/3oz	110g/4oz	140g/5oz	170g/6oz	225g/8oz	340g/12oz	500g/1lb 2oz	750g/1lb 11oz
currants	55g/2oz	55g/2oz	70g/2½oz	85g/3oz	110g/4oz	170g/6oz	250g/9oz	370g/13oz
mixed peel	30g/1oz	30g/1oz	45g/1½oz	45g/1½oz	55g/2oz	85g/3oz	170g/6oz	250g/9oz
glacé cherries	30g/1oz	30g/1oz	45g/1½oz	45g/1½oz	55g/2oz	85g/3oz	170g/6oz	250g/9oz
dried apricots	70g/2½oz	85g/3oz	110g/4oz	140g/5oz	170g/6oz	285g/10oz	450g/1lb	675g/1½lb
dried apples	30g/1oz	30g/1oz	45g/1½oz	45g/1½oz	55g/2oz	85g/3oz	170g/6oz	250g/9oz
dried dates	45g/1½oz	55g/2oz	70g/2½oz	85g/3oz	110g/4oz	170g/6oz	250g/9oz	370g/13oz
dried peaches	45g/1½oz	55g/2oz	70g/2½oz	85g/3oz	110g/4oz	170g/6oz	250g/9oz	370g/13oz
dried pears	45g/1½oz	55g/2oz	70g/2½oz	85g/3oz	110g/4oz	170g/6oz	250g/9oz	370g/13oz
butter	85g/3oz	110g/4oz	140g/5oz	170g/6oz	225g/8oz	340g/12oz	500g/1lb 2oz	750g/1lb 11oz
soft brown sugar	85g/3oz	110g/4oz	140g/5oz	170g/6oz	225g/8oz	340g/12oz	500g/1lb 2oz	750g/1lg 11oz
lemon (juice and rind)	½	½	1	1	1	2	3	3½
orange (juice and rind)	½	½	1	1	1	2	3	3½
water	45ml/1½fl oz	55ml/2fl oz	70ml/2½fl oz	85ml/3fl oz	110ml/4fl oz	170ml/6fl oz	250ml/9fl oz	370ml/13fl oz
orange juice	45ml/1½fl oz	55ml/2fl oz	70ml/2½fl oz	85ml/3fl oz	110ml/4fl oz	170ml/6fl oz	250ml/9fl oz	370ml/13fl oz
brandy	45ml/1½fl oz	55ml/2fl oz	70ml/2½fl oz	85ml/3fl oz	110ml/4fl oz	170ml/6fl oz	250ml/9fl oz	370ml/13fl oz
grated nutmeg	⅛ teasp	¼ teasp	¼ teasp	½ teasp	½ teasp	1 teasp	1½ teasp	2 teasp
ground cinnamon	¼ teasp	½ teasp	½ teasp	1 teasp	1 teasp	2 teasp	3 teasp	4 teasp
ground allspice	¼ teasp	½ teasp	½ teasp	1 teasp	1 teasp	2 teasp	3 teasp	4 teasp
ground ginger	⅛ teasp	¼ teasp	¼ teasp	½ teasp	½ teasp	1 teasp	1½ teasp	2 teasp
ground cardamom	pinch	⅛ teasp	⅛ teasp	¼ teasp	¼ teasp	½ teasp	1 teasp	1½ teasp
black treacle	¼ tblsp	½ tblsp	½ tblsp	1 tblsp	2 tblsp	2 tblsp	3 teasp	4 teasp
eggs	2	2½	3	4	5	8	11	14
plain flour	140g/5oz	170g/6 oz	225g/8oz	250g/9oz	310g/11oz	500g/1lb 2oz	750g/1lb 11oz	1kg/2¼lb
baking powder	¼ teasp	½ teasp	½ teasp	1 teasp	1 teasp	2 teasp	2½ teasp	3½ teasp
baking time	2–2½ hours	2¾ hours	3¼ hours	3½–4 hours	4–4½ hours	4½–5 hours	5–5½ hours	6–6½ hours

Cakes with fresh fruit

♦ ♦

Cider Cake

melted lard or oil for greasing tin
170g/6oz butter
170g/6oz soft light brown sugar
3 eggs, beaten
170g/6oz self-raising flour, sifted
½ teaspoon freshly grated nutmeg
2 tablespoons medium sweet cider
2 dessert apples, such as Cox's Orange Pippins,
    peeled, quartered, cored and sliced
¼ teaspoon ground cinnamon
½ teaspoon demerara sugar

1. Preheat the oven to 180°C/350°F/gas
mark 4. Grease a 900g/2lb loaf tin and line
with a piece of greased greaseproof paper.
2. Cream the butter and soft light brown
sugar together in a mixing bowl until light
and fluffy. Add the eggs gradually, beating
well after each addition. Add a little of the
flour if necessary to prevent the mixture
from curdling.
3. Fold the sifted flour and nutmeg into the
creamed mixture, using a large metal spoon,
and stir in the cider. Turn into the prepared
tin and spread out evenly.
4. Bake in the centre of the oven for 20
minutes.
5. Remove the cake from the oven and
quickly arrange the sliced apples over the
top. Sprinkle with the cinnamon and
demerara sugar mixed together. Work
quickly, otherwise the cake will sink. When
the cake is baked, the apples will have sunk
slightly into the crust.
6. Return the cake to the oven and bake for
30 further minutes or until a sharp knife or
skewer inserted into the centre of the cake
comes out clean.
7. Remove the cake from the oven and
allow to cool completely in the tin before
turning out.

♦ ♦

Apple Cake

melted lard or oil for greasing tin
225g/8oz plain flour
2 teaspoons baking powder
110g/4oz butter
110g/4oz granulated sugar
225g/8oz dessert apples, such as Cox's Orange
    Pippins, peeled, cored and diced

85g/3oz raisins
1 egg
100ml/3½fl oz milk
45g/1½oz demerara sugar

1. Preheat the oven to 180°C/350°F/gas
mark 4. Grease a 20cm/7in deep cake tin
and line the base with a disc of greased
greaseproof paper.

2. Sift the flour with the baking powder into a large mixing bowl. Cut the butter into small cubes and rub into the flour until the mixture resembles fine breadcrumbs.

3. Add the granulated sugar, apples and raisins and mix thoroughly.

4. Mix together the egg and milk and add to the mixture. It should form a reluctant dropping consistency. Add more milk if necessary. Turn into the prepared tin.

5. Bake in the centre of the oven for 40 minutes, then reduce the temperature to 170°C/325°F/gas mark 3 and bake for about 50 further minutes or until a sharp knife or skewer inserted into the centre of the cake comes out clean.

6. Remove from the oven and immediately sprinkle with the demerara sugar. Allow to cool in the tin for 30 minutes, then turn out on to a wire rack and leave to cool completely.

◆ ◆

Cheese and Apple Cake

melted lard or oil for greasing tin
110g/4oz butter
170g/6oz caster sugar
2 eggs, beaten
225g/8oz cored and unpeeled cooking apples,
*   grated with peel and juice*
110g/4oz Cheddar cheese, grated
55g/2oz blanched almonds, chopped
450g/1lb plain flour
2 teaspoons baking powder
½ teaspoon bicarbonate of soda

1. Preheat the oven to 180°C/350°F/gas mark 4. Grease a 900g/2lb loaf tin and line the base with a piece of greased greaseproof paper.

2. Cream the butter and sugar together in a mixing bowl, until light and fluffy. Add the eggs gradually, beating well after each addition. Stir in the apples, cheese and almonds.

3. Sift together the flour, baking powder and bicarbonate of soda and fold into the mixture, using a large metal spoon.

4. Turn into the prepared tin. Smooth the top with a palette knife.

5. Bake in the centre of the oven for about 1 hour or until a sharp knife or skewer inserted into the centre of the cake comes out clean.

6. Remove the cake from the oven and allow to cool in the tin for 10 minutes, then turn out on to a wire rack and leave to cool completely.

◆ ◆

Normandy Apple Cake

For the filling
3 cooking apples, total weight about 450g/1lb
15g/½oz butter
a strip of thinly pared lemon zest
about 85g/3oz soft light brown sugar

For the cake
melted lard or oil for greasing tin
125g/4½oz caster sugar
40g/1½oz ground hazelnuts, toasted until brown
4 egg yolks
50g/1¾oz plain flour
50g/1¾oz arrowroot
3 egg whites

To serve
icing sugar, sifted
50ml/5fl oz double cream, whipped

1. Wash but do not peel the apples, quarter and core them, then slice thinly. Melt the butter in a heavy saucepan and add the apples with the lemon zest and 4 tablespoons water. Cover with a lid and cook over a gentle heat, stirring occasionally, until completely soft. Push through a sieve.

2. Return the measured purée to the rinsed-out pan. Add at least 55g/2oz sugar to 570ml/1 pint purée. Cook rapidly for about 4 minutes until the mixture is of a dropping consistency. Remove from the heat and leave to cool.

3. Preheat the oven to 180°C/350°F/gas mark 4. Grease a 20cm/8in sandwich tin or moule-à-manqué and dust lightly with flour. Tap out the excess.

4. Beat the sugar, nuts and egg yolks together in a mixing bowl until white and creamy. Sift the flour with the arrowroot and fold into the creamed mixture, using a large metal spoon.

5. Whisk the egg whites until stiff but not dry and fold them into the mixture. Turn into the prepared tin and spread out evenly.

6. Bake in the centre of the oven for 40 minutes or until the top springs back when pressed lightly with a fingertip.

7. Remove the cake from the oven and allow to cool in the tin for 10 minutes, then turn out on to a wire rack and leave to cool completely.

8. When the cake is cold, split in half horizontally and sandwich together with the apple filling. Dredge the top with icing sugar. Serve with the cream.

◆ ◆

Apple Sauce Cake

This cake is moist and keeps very well. It does not contain eggs and is therefore fairly close-textured.

melted lard or oil for greasing tin
340g/12oz cooking apples
110g/4oz butter
225g/8oz caster sugar
225g/8oz plain flour, sifted
1 teaspoon ground mixed spice
1 teaspoon bicarbonate of soda
170g/6oz dried apricots, chopped
1 tablespoon demerara sugar

1. Preheat the oven to 180°C/350°F/gas mark 4. Grease an 15cm/7in cake tin and line the base with a disc of greased greaseproof paper.

2. Wash but do not peel the apples, core them and cut into chunks. Put them into a saucepan with 1 tablespoon water. Cover with a lid and cook over a low heat, stirring occasionally, until pulpy. Push the apples through a sieve and set aside to cool.

3. Meanwhile, cream the butter in a mixing bowl and add the caster sugar. Beat together until soft and creamy.

4. Add the cooled apple purée, flour, mixed spice, bicarbonate of soda and dried apricots. Mix well. Turn into the prepared tin.

5. Bake in the centre of the oven for about 1½ hours or until a sharp knife or skewer inserted into the centre of the cake comes out clean. 10 minutes before the end of baking time, sprinkle with the demerara sugar.

6. Remove the cake from the oven and allow to cool in the tin for 10 minutes, then turn out on to a wire rack and leave to cool completely.

NOTE: This cake can also be baked in a 900g/2lb loaf tin.

♦ ♦

Spiced Ginger Roll

This is a delicious cake to serve as a pudding, to serve 4, or for tea. You need to eat it with a fork.

For the filling
375g/12oz cooking apples
30g/1oz butter
1 teaspoon ground cinnamon
55g/2oz sugar

For the roll
melted lard or oil for greasing tin
110g/4oz plain flour
1 teaspoon ground mixed spice
1 teaspoon ground ginger
70g/2½oz butter
2 tablespoons black treacle
2 tablespoons golden syrup
1 egg
150ml/5fl oz water

1 teaspoon bicarbonate of soda
caster sugar

To serve
150ml/5fl oz double cream, whipped

1. First make the filling: peel and core the apples. Slice them thickly.

2. Melt the butter in a saucepan and add the cinnamon, sugar and apples. Cover with a lid and cook over a very gentle heat, stirring occasionally, until the apples are pulpy. Remove from the heat and beat until smooth, adding more sugar if the apples are still tart. Allow to cool.

3. Preheat the oven to 180°C/350°F/gas mark 4. Grease a 30 × 23cm/12 × 9in Swiss roll tin and line the base with greased greaseproof paper. Dust with caster sugar. Tap out the excess.

4. Make the roll: sift the flour, mixed spice and ginger together into a mixing bowl. Melt the butter in a saucepan with the treacle and syrup. Do not allow to boil. Remove from heat. Whisk the egg with the water and

bicarbonate of soda and add to the melted mixture.

5. Pour the mixture into the flour and whisk together for 30 seconds. Pour into the prepared dish.

6. Bake in the centre of the oven for 12–15 minutes or until firm to the touch.

7. Turn out on to a sheet of greaseproof paper dusted with caster sugar. Remove the lining paper. Spread the cake with the apple purée, roll up like a Swiss roll (see page 33) and serve with the cream.

♦ ♦

Spiced Pear and Ginger Upside-down Cake

Pears and ginger go very well together and this can be served as a cake or warm as a pudding, to serve 4–6.

For the topping
3 dessert pears, peeled, halved and cored
570ml/1 pint sugar syrup (see page 143)
55g/2oz butter
55g/2oz soft light brown sugar

For the cake
melted lard or oil for greasing tin
110g/4oz butter
110g/4oz soft dark brown sugar
170g/6oz black treacle
225g/8oz plain flour
2 teaspoons ground ginger
2 eggs, beaten
85ml/3fl oz milk
1 teaspoon bicarbonate of soda

To serve
290ml/½ pint Greek yoghurt

1. Preheat the oven to 180°C/350°F/gas mark 4. Grease a 20cm/8in deep cake tin.

2. Make the topping: poach the pears in the sugar syrup in a large saucepan for 30 minutes until soft.

3. Cream the butter and light brown sugar together in a bowl until soft and light. Spread on the base of the prepared tin. Place the pears, cut sides down, on top of the butter and sugar mixture with the tops pointing inwards.

4. Make the cake: melt the butter in a saucepan with the dark brown sugar and treacle. Do not allow to boil. Remove from the heat and allow to cool a little.

5. Sift the flour with the ginger into a large mixing bowl. Make a well in the centre and pour in the eggs and the treacle mixture. Mix the flour in carefully to make a smooth batter.

6. Warm the milk gently, add the bicarbonate of soda and pour into the batter. Mix well. Pour the mixture carefully over the pears in the tin, making sure they are not dislodged.

7. Bake in the oven for about 45 minutes or until a sharp knife or skewer inserted into the centre of the cake comes out clean.

8. Remove the cake from the oven and allow to cool in the tin for a few minutes, then turn upside-down on to a plate. Serve warm, cut into wedges, with the yoghurt.

◆◆◆◆◆◆◆◆◆◆◆◆◆◆◆◆◆◆◆◆◆◆

Pear and Ginger Muffins

You will need 10 paper muffin cases or a muffin tin for these American-style muffins.

MAKES 10

melted lard or oil for greasing tins
110g/4oz butter
55g/2oz honey
140g/5oz soft light brown sugar
2 medium pears, peeled, cored and roughly
* chopped*
70g/2½oz pecan nuts, roughly chopped
225g/8oz plain flour
1 teaspoon bicarbonate of soda
1 teaspoon ground cinnamon
½ teaspoon freshly grated nutmeg
½ teaspoon ground cloves

a pinch of salt
2 small eggs, beaten

1. Preheat the oven to 180°C/350°F/gas mark 4. Grease 10 muffin tins or put 10 muffin cases on to a baking sheet.
2. Melt the butter in a saucepan with the honey and sugar. Do not allow to boil.
3. Toss the pears and nuts in the butter and honey mixture.
4. Sift together the flour, bicarbonate of soda, spices and salt.
5. Add the eggs to the butter and pear mixture. Fold in the flour. Fill the muffin tins or cases to the top with the mixture.
6. Bake in the top of the oven for 35–40 minutes or until the muffins spring back when pressed lightly with a fingertip. Transfer to a wire rack and leave to cool.

◆◆◆◆◆◆◆◆◆◆◆◆◆◆◆◆◆◆◆◆◆◆

Blueberry Muffins

These muffins are very easy to make. If blueberries are hard to find, try fresh or frozen raspberries or blackcurrants. You will need 12 paper muffin cases or muffin tins.

MAKES 12

melted lard or oil for greasing tins
340g/12oz plain flour
3 teaspoons baking powder
½ teaspoon salt
110g/4oz caster sugar

290ml/½ pint milk
1 egg, lightly beaten
55g/2oz butter, melted and cooled
225g/8oz blueberries (fresh or frozen)

1. Preheat the oven to 200°C/400°F/gas mark 6. Grease 12 muffin tins or put 12 muffin cases on to a baking sheet.
2. Sift the flour, baking powder, salt and sugar together into a large mixing bowl. Make a well in the centre.
3. Mix together the milk, egg and butter. Pour the mixture gradually into the well,

mixing well with a wooden spoon and incorporating the flour as you stir, to make a smooth batter.

4. Mix in the blueberries lightly and spoon into the muffin tins or cases, filling each one by no more than two-thirds.

5. Bake in the centre of the oven for about 25–30 minutes or until well risen and brown.

6. Transfer the muffins to a wire rack and leave to cool.

◆ ◆

Orange Muffins

You will need 16 paper muffin cases or muffin tins.

MAKES 16
melted lard or oil for greasing tins
340g/12oz plain flour
1 teaspoon bicarbonate of soda
finely grated zest of 2 oranges
225g/8oz caster sugar
2 eggs, beaten
110g/4oz butter, melted and cooled
290ml/10fl oz natural yoghurt
110g/4oz raisins

1. Preheat the oven to 200°C/400°F/gas mark 6. Grease 16 muffin tins or put 16 muffin cases on to a baking sheet.

2. Sift the flour with the bicarbonate of soda into a large mixing bowl. Add the orange zest and sugar. Make a well in the centre.

3. Put the eggs, butter and yoghurt into the well and gradually incorporate all the flour, mixing to a smooth batter.

4. Stir in the raisins and spoon into the muffin tins or cases, filling each by no more than two-thirds.

5. Bake in the centre of the oven for 20–25 minutes or until the muffins spring back when pressed lightly with a fingertip.

6. Transfer to a wire rack and leave to cool.

◆ ◆

Date Cake

The date layer in this cake tends to sink to the bottom, making it slightly sticky and delicious.

For the cake
melted lard or oil for greasing tin
110g/4oz butter
110g/4oz caster sugar
1 egg, beaten
1 teaspoon vanilla essence
110g/4oz plain flour
1½ teaspoons baking powder
150ml/5fl oz milk

For the date layer
110g/4oz dried dates, chopped
85g/3oz light soft brown sugar
1 tablespoon plain flour
2 teaspoons ground cinnamon
55g/2oz butter, melted and cooled

For the top
55g/2oz hazelnuts, chopped

1. Preheat the oven to 180°C/350°F/gas mark 4. Grease a 15cm/6in square cake tin and line the base with a piece of greased greaseproof paper.

2. Cream the butter and sugar together in a mixing bowl until light and fluffy. Add the egg gradually, beating well after each addition. Add the vanilla essence.

3. Sift the flour with the baking powder and fold into the mixture, using a large metal spoon. Stir in the milk.

4. Mix together the ingredients for the date layer.

5. Spread half the cake mixture in the bottom of the prepared tin. Spoon the date layer mixture carefully on top, spreading it out evenly, and spread the remaining cake mixture over that. Sprinkle over the hazelnuts and press down lightly.

6. Bake in the centre of the top oven for about 45 minutes or until the top springs back when pressed lightly with a fingertip.

7. Remove the cake from the oven and allow to cool completely in the tin before turning out.

♦ ♦

Date and Orange Loaf

The recipe for this delicious loaf was given to me by Babs Stevenson, an ex-Principal of Leith's School of Food and Wine. It improves greatly on keeping and is very good served spread with butter.

melted lard or oil for greasing tin
225g/8oz dried dates, chopped
110ml/4fl oz water
170g/6oz soft dark brown sugar
170g/6oz butter
grated zest of 1 orange
2 tablespoons orange juice
1 egg, beaten
225g/8oz plain flour
1 teaspoon baking powder
1 teaspoon ground allspice

1. Preheat the oven to 160°C/325°F/gas mark 3. Grease a 675g/1½lb loaf tin and line the base with a piece of greased greaseproof paper.

2. Put the dates into a small saucepan, add the water and bring to the boil. Cover with a lid and simmer for 5 minutes or until the dates are soft and pulpy.

3. Add the sugar, butter, orange zest and juice and beat well off the heat until the butter has melted and everything is well amalgamated.

4. Allow the melted mixture to cool, then add the egg.

5. Sift together the flour, baking powder and allspice and add gradually to the melted mixture. Mix well until smooth. Pour into the prepared tin.

6. Bake in the centre of the oven for 1–1½ hours or until the top springs back when pressed lightly with a fingertip.

7. Remove the cake from the oven and allow to cool in the tin for 15 minutes, then turn out on to a wire rack and leave to cool completely.

8. Keep the loaf for 1 day to soften before cutting.

◆◆◆◆◆◆◆◆◆◆◆◆◆◆◆◆◆◆◆◆◆◆

Cranberry and Pecan Cake

melted lard or oil for greasing tin
225g/8oz butter
225g/8oz soft light brown sugar
225g/8oz golden syrup
340g/12oz plain flour
½ teaspoon ground cinnamon
½ teaspoon ground coriander
½ teaspoon ground ginger
½ teaspoon ground mace
2 eggs, beaten
grated zest of 1 orange
290ml/½ pint milk
2 teaspoons bicarbonate of soda
225/8oz cranberries, crushed very lightly with a
　　fork
85g/3oz pecan nuts, chopped

1. Preheat the oven to 150°C/300°F/gas
mark 2. Grease a 22cm/9in deep cake tin
and line the base with a disc of greased
greaseproof paper.
 2. Melt the butter with the sugar and syrup
in a saucepan. Do not allow to boil. Remove
from the heat and allow to cool.
3. Sift the flour and spices together into a
large mixing bowl. Make a well in the centre
and pour in the melted mixture, the eggs and
orange zest. Mix well.
4. Warm the milk and add the bicarbonate
of soda. Mix into the cake mixture with the
cranberries and nuts. Turn into the prepared
tin.
5. Bake in the centre of the oven for about 2
hours or until a sharp knife or skewer
inserted into the centre of the cake comes
out clean.
6. Remove the cake from the oven and
allow to cool completely in the tin before
turning out.

◆◆◆◆◆◆◆◆◆◆◆◆◆◆◆◆◆◆◆◆◆◆

Squashy Rhubarb Cake

This cake can also be served as a winter
pudding, to serve 4, accompanied by *crème
anglaise* or double cream.

For the crumble topping
55g/2oz butter
85g/3oz plain flour
30g/1oz sugar

For the cake
melted lard or oil for greasing tin
85g/3oz butter
85g/3oz sugar
2 small eggs, beaten
85g/3oz self-raising flour, sifted with a pinch of
　　salt
milk

For the filling
675g/1½lb rhubarb, cut into 2.5cm/1in pieces
1 tablespoon sugar

Battenburg Cake

Dobez Torte

Upside-down Toffee Gingerbread

Christening Cake

Old-fashioned Boiled Christmas Cake

Squashy Rhubarb Cake

Lemon Sponge Syrup Cake and Orange and Poppy Seed Cake

Chocolate Polenta Cake

To finish
icing sugar, sifted

1. Preheat the oven to 190°C/375°F/gas mark 5. Grease a 20cm/8in loose-bottomed cake tin.
2. Make the crumble topping: rub the butter into the flour in a bowl and add the sugar. Set aside.
3. Make the cake: cream the butter in a mixing bowl until soft. Add the sugar and cream until very pale, light and fluffy.
4. Add the eggs gradually to the mixture, beating well after each addition. Add a spoonful of the flour if necessary, to prevent the mixture from curdling.
5. Fold in the flour, using a large metal spoon, and add a few dribbles of milk if necessary, to achieve a reluctant dropping consistency.
6. Turn into the prepared tin and spread out evenly flat. Cover carefully with the rhubarb pieces tossed in the sugar. Sprinkle with the crumble mixture.
7. Bake in the centre of the oven for about 45 minutes or until the top feels firm to the touch.
8. Remove the cake from the oven and allow to cool completely in the tin before turning out.
9. Just before serving, remove the cake from the tin and dust with icing sugar.

NOTE: Tinned rhubarb may be used, without the sugar. You will need a 450g/1lb tin, drained.

♦ ♦

Fresh Fruit Cake

melted lard or oil for greasing tin
225g/8oz mixed fresh fruit, such as apples,
   pears, plums, nectarines
170g/6oz butter
170g/6oz caster sugar
3 eggs, beaten
170g/6oz self-raising flour
2 teaspoons ground cinnamon

1. Preheat the oven to 180°C/350°F/gas mark 4. Grease a 20cm/8in deep cake tin and line the base with a disc of greased greaseproof paper.
2. Peel, core and stone the fruit. Cut into 1cm/½in dice.
3. Cream the butter and sugar together in a mixing bowl until light and fluffy. Add the eggs gradually, beating well after each addition. Add a little of the flour if necessary, to prevent the mixture from curdling.
4. Sift the flour with the cinnamon and fold into the creamed mixture with the chopped fruit. Turn into the prepared tin.
5. Bake in the centre of the oven for 1 hour or until the top feels firm to the touch.
6. Remove the cake from the oven and allow to cool in the tin for 10 minutes, then turn out on to a wire rack and leave to cool completely.

♦ ♦

Nectarine Cake

This is a pretty, sticky cake that can also be served warm as a pudding, to serve 4. Peaches can be used instead of nectarines but you will need to peel them by dunking them in boiling water for 20 seconds, then in cold water.

3 ripe nectarines
1 tablespoon lemon juice
55g/2oz butter
55g/2oz sugar
1 egg, beaten
140g/5oz self-raising flour, sifted
55ml/2fl oz milk
3 tablespoons apricot jam

1. Preheat the oven to 180°C/350°F/gas mark 4. Grease a 20cm/8in loose-bottomed flan tin.
2. Cut each unpeeled nectarine into about 16 segments. Toss in the lemon juice.
3. Cream the butter and sugar together in a mixing bowl until light and fluffy. Add the egg gradually, beating well after each addition. Fold the flour into the mixture. Add the milk, mixing carefully.
4. Spread into the prepared tin and arrange the segments of nectarine on top as neatly as possible, pressing them lightly into the cake mixture.
5. Bake in the centre of the oven for 50–60 minutes or until a sharp knife or skewer inserted into the centre comes out clean.
6. Meanwhile, put the apricot jam into a saucepan with 1 tablespoon water. Bring to the boil, then push through a sieve.
7. Remove the cake from the oven and allow to cool in the tin for 15 minutes, then turn out on to a wire rack and leave to cool completely. Brush the top with the warm apricot glaze. Allow to cool.

◆◆◆◆◆◆◆◆◆◆◆◆◆◆◆◆◆◆◆◆◆◆

Passionfruit Cake

The passionfruit in this recipe should be ripe, which means they will have a wrinkled, slightly sunken skin. Unripe passionfruit are plump and firm and have a very sour taste.

melted lard or oil for greasing tin
225g/8oz butter
225g/8oz caster sugar
4 eggs, beaten
225g/8oz self-raising flour, sifted
2 ripe passionfruit

For the filling
6 tablespoons passionfruit curd (see page 155)

For the icing
1-passionfruit quantity passionfruit icing (see page 140)

1. Preheat the oven to 190°C/375°F/gas mark 5. Grease two 20cm/8in sandwich tins and line the base of each with a disc of greased greaseproof paper.
2. Cream the butter in a mixing bowl, add the sugar and beat together until pale and creamy.
3. Add the eggs gradually, beating well after each addition. Add a little of the flour if necessary, to prevent the mixture from curdling. Fold in the remaining flour, using a large metal spoon.

4. Cut open the passionfruit and scoop out the pulp. Fold into the creamed mixture. Divide the mixture between the sandwich tins and spread out evenly.

5. Bake in the centre of the oven for 35–40 minutes or until the tops spring back when pressed lightly with a fingertip.

6. Meanwhile, make the passionfruit curd and passionfruit icing.

7. Remove the cake from the oven and allow to cool in the tin for 5 minutes, then turn out on to a wire rack and leave to cool completely.

8. When the cakes are cold, sandwich together with the passionfruit curd and spread the top with the passionfruit icing. Allow to set.

NOTE: This cake will keep for a day or so in a tin in a cool place. It will also freeze quite successfully although the glacé icing might become a bit wet on defrosting.

3 CITRUS CAKES

Other cakes in this book have some citrus fruit as an ingredient but those in this chapter have a particularly tangy citrus flavour. This is true of the syrup cakes, for example, which are very easy to make, taste wonderful, freeze beautifully and are therefore a very useful addition to a cake maker's repertoire.

◆ ◆

Citrus Sponge Cake

oil for greasing tin
225g/8oz butter
225g/8oz caster sugar
finely grated zest and juice of 2 limes
finely grated zest and juice of 1 lemon
finely grated zest and juice of 1 orange
4 eggs, beaten
225g/8oz self-raising flour
55g/2oz ground almonds
1 tablespoon caster sugar

For the topping
170g/6oz curd cheese
reserved grated zest
icing sugar, sifted

1. Preheat the oven to 190°C/375°F/gas mark 5. Oil a 22cm/9in round or 20cm/8in square deep cake tin and line the base with a piece of oiled greaseproof paper.

2. Cream the butter and sugar together in a mixing bowl until light and fluffy. Reserve 1 tablespoon of the mixed citrus zest and beat the remainder into the creamed mixture.
3. Add the eggs gradually, beating well after each addition. Add a little of the flour if necessary, to prevent the mixture from curdling. Beat very well.
4. Fold in the remaining flour and the ground almonds to achieve a reluctant dropping consistency, adding a little water if necessary. Turn into the prepared tin.
5. Bake in the centre of the oven for 20–25 minutes or until well risen and golden and the top springs back when pressed lightly with a fingertip.
6. Remove from the oven and allow to cool in the tin for a few minutes, then turn out on to a wire rack and pierce the top all over with a skewer.
7. Mix the lime, lemon and orange juices with the sugar in a small bowl and drizzle over the top of the cake while still warm. Leave to cool completely.

8. When the cake is cold, make the topping: put the curd cheese into a bowl with the reserved citrus zest and beat with a wooden spoon until soft and creamy. Add icing sugar to taste. Spread evenly over the cake with a palette knife.

◆ ◆

Lemon and Orange-flower Cake

melted lard or oil for greasing tin
5 eggs
170g/6oz caster sugar
1½ tablespoons orangeflower water
juice and finely grated zest of 1 lemon
170g/6oz plain flour
¼ teaspoon baking powder
55g/2oz butter, melted and cooled

To serve
3 tablespoons lemon curd (see page 154)
icing sugar, sifted

1. Preheat the oven to 180°C/350°F/gas mark 4. Grease a 20cm/8in moule-à-manqué tin and line the base with a disc of greased greaseproof paper.
2. Separate the eggs and whisk the yolks and 85g/3oz of the sugar in a large bowl until very light and pale. Whisk in the orangeflower water and lemon zest and juice.
3. In a second large bowl whisk the egg whites until stiff. Whisk in the remaining sugar gradually until very thick and shiny.
4. Sift the flour with the baking powder.
5. Half-fold the egg whites into the yolk mixture, using a large metal spoon. Add the butter, flour and baking powder and fold together carefully. Pour into the prepared tin.
6. Bake in the centre of the oven for about 35 minutes or until the top springs back when pressed lightly with a fingertip. Loosen the sides of the cake with a knife, turn out on to a wire rack and leave to cool completely.
7. When the cake is cold, split it in half horizontally and sandwich together with the lemon curd. Dust with icing sugar.

◆ ◆

Summer Lemon Cake

melted lard or oil for greasing tins
6 eggs
170g/6oz caster sugar
2 tablespoons water
finely grated zest of 1 lemon
85g/3oz plain flour
30g/1oz cornflour

For the lemon filling
290ml/½ pint double cream
5 tablespoons lemon curd (see page 154)
110g/4oz almonds, chopped and toasted

1. Preheat the oven to 180°C/350°F/gas mark 4. Grease two 20cm/8in sandwich tins and line the base of each with a disc of greased greaseproof paper.
2. Separate the eggs and put the yolks, sugar, water and lemon zest into a heatproof bowl. Fit over (not in) a saucepan of gently simmering water and whisk until light and fluffy. (If using an electric beater, no heat is required.)
3. Sift the flour and cornflour together and fold into the yolk mixture carefully, using a large metal spoon.
4. Whisk the egg whites until stiff and fold into the mixture. Divide between the prepared tins and spread out evenly.
5. Bake in the centre of the oven for 45 minutes or until the tops spring back when pressed lightly with a fingertip.
6. Remove from the oven and allow to cool in the tins for 10 minutes, then turn out on to a wire rack and leave to cool completely.
7. Meanwhile, make the filling: whisk the cream until it just holds its shape and add the lemon curd. Continue whisking until stiff, but do not overwhip or the mixture will curdle. Add more lemon curd if you like a pronounced lemony flavour.
8. When the cakes are cold, sandwich them together with some of the filling and spread the top and sides with the remainder. Press the almonds over the top and sides of the cake and keep in the refrigerator until required.

♦ ♦

Lemon Sponge Syrup Cake

melted lard or oil for greasing tin
170g/6oz butter
170g/6oz caster sugar
finely grated zest of 1 lemon
3 eggs, beaten
170g/6oz self-raising flour, sifted
4 tablespoons milk

For the lemon syrup
4 tablespoons fresh lemon juice
4 tablespoons icing sugar, sifted

1. Preheat the oven to 180°C/350°F/gas mark 4. Grease a 900g/2lb loaf tin and line the base with a piece of greased greaseproof paper.
2. Cream the butter and sugar together in a mixing bowl until light and fluffy. Beat in the lemon zest. Add the eggs gradually, beating well after each addition. Add a little of the flour if necessary to prevent the mixture from curdling.
3. Fold in the remaining flour, using a large metal spoon. Add the milk and mix to a soft dropping consistency. Turn into the prepared tin and smooth the top.
4. Bake in the centre of the oven for 40–45 minutes or until the top springs back when pressed lightly with a fingertip.
5. Meanwhile, mix the lemon juice with the icing sugar. Pour over the cake as soon as it is removed from the oven. Allow to cool completely in the tin before turning out.

♦ ♦

Yoghurt Cake with Lemon Syrup

This cake is steeped in lemon syrup for up to 24 hours after it has been baked. It tastes fresh and very delicious.

melted lard or oil for greasing tin
85g/3oz self-raising flour, sifted
a pinch of salt
1 teaspoon baking powder
225g/8oz semolina
140g/5oz caster sugar
150ml/5fl oz sunflower oil
250g/9oz Greek yoghurt
1 teaspoon vanilla essence
1 tablespoon orange-flower water
2 eggs, beaten
55g/2oz hazelnuts, toasted and finely chopped

For the syrup
170g/6oz caster sugar
juice of 1 lemon
290ml/½ pint water

1. Preheat the oven to 190°C/375°F/gas mark 5. Lightly oil a 20cm/8in cake tin and line the base with a disc of greased greaseproof paper.

2. Sift the flour again, with the salt and baking powder, into a large mixing bowl and mix in the semolina and sugar. Make a well in the centre.

3. Mix together the oil, yoghurt, vanilla essence, orange-flower water and eggs and pour into the well. Using a wooden spoon, gradually draw in the dry ingredients from the sides, and beat until smooth. Pour into the prepared tin, spread out evenly and sprinkle with the hazelnuts.

4. Bake in the centre of the oven for 35–40 minutes or until a sharp knife inserted into the centre comes out clean. Remove from the oven and leave to cool in the tin for 10 minutes.

5. Meanwhile, make the syrup: put the sugar and lemon juice into a small saucepan. Add the water and stir over a low heat without boiling until the sugar has dissolved completely. Bring to the boil, then reduce the heat and simmer for 5 minutes. Turn off the heat but keep the syrup warm.

6. Turn the cake out on to a plate while still warm. Pierce the top with a skewer in about 12–15 different places and spoon over the syrup. Leave the cake to cool and soak up the syrup for 24 hours, spooning the syrup over from time to time so that as much as possible is absorbed.

♦ ♦

Passionfruit and Lime Syrup Cake

melted lard or oil for greasing tin
170g/6oz butter
170g/6oz caster sugar
grated zest of ½ lime
3 large eggs, beaten
170g/6oz self-raising flour, sifted
water

For the syrup
juice of 2 limes
3 passionfruit, halved, juice and seeds reserved
55g/2oz caster sugar

1. Preheat the oven to 190°C/375°F/gas mark 5. Grease a 30 × 20cm/12 × 8in shallow cake tin and line the base with a piece of greased greaseproof paper.
2. Cream the butter in a mixing bowl until soft, then add the sugar and beat until light and fluffy. Add the lime zest.
3. Add the eggs gradually, beating well after each addition. Add a little of the flour if necessary to prevent the mixture from curdling.
4. Fold in the remaining flour, using a large metal spoon. Add enough water to achieve a dropping consistency. Turn into the prepared tin and spread out evenly.
5. Bake in the centre of the oven for about 20 minutes or until well risen and golden and the top springs back when pressed lightly with a fingertip.
6. Lay a piece of greaseproof paper on the work surface. Loosen the edges of the cake and turn it out on to the paper. Peel away the lining paper from the bottom of the cake. Turn the right way up on to a wire rack.
7. Make the syrup: put the sugar and lime juice into a small saucepan and stir over a low heat without boiling until the sugar has dissolved completely.
8. Bring to the boil and boil until syrupy. Remove from the heat and allow to cool slightly, then add the passionfruit pulp and seeds.
9. While the cake is still warm, brush the top liberally with the syrup. Leave to cool. The syrup will harden to a crust.

◆◆◆◆◆◆◆◆◆◆◆◆◆◆◆◆◆◆◆◆◆◆◆

Orange and Poppy Seed Cake

melted lard or oil for greasing tin
110g/4oz butter
225g/8oz sugar
4 eggs, beaten
225g/8oz plain flour
2½ teaspoons baking powder
150ml/5fl oz milk
85g/3oz poppy seeds
1 teaspoon vanilla essence
finely grated zest of 2 oranges

For the glaze
110ml/4fl oz fresh orange juice
110g/4oz granulated sugar

1. Preheat the oven to 160°C/325°F/gas mark 3. Grease a 23cm/9½in loose-bottomed cake tin and line the base with a

disc of greased greaseproof paper.

2. Cream the butter and sugar together in a mixing bowl until light and fluffy. Add the eggs gradually, beating well after each addition. Add a little of the flour if necessary to prevent the mixture from curdling.

3. Sift the remaining flour with the baking powder on to the creamed mixture. Using a large metal spoon, fold in carefully, adding the milk, poppy seeds, vanilla essence and orange zest. Pour into the prepared tin.

4. Bake in the centre of the oven for 1–1¼ hours or until the top springs back when pressed lightly with a fingertip. Cover with a piece of greaseproof paper if the top is getting too dark.

5. Meanwhile, make the glaze by combining the orange juice and sugar in a small saucepan. Bring to the boil, then reduce the heat and simmer for 5 minutes

6. Remove the cake from the oven and allow to cool in the tin for 30 minutes, then turn out on to a wire rack to cool. While still warm, prick holes all over the top with a skewer and pour over the warm glaze. Leave to cool completely.

◆ ◆

Bitter Orange Cake

This unusual cake, which takes some time to prepare, contains no flour and so is good for people on a gluten-free diet. It is delicious served as a pudding or with orange curd (see page 154) as a tea-time cake.

2 small thin-skinned oranges
285g/10oz whole blanched almonds
melted lard or oil for greasing tin
5 eggs
225g/8oz caster sugar
1 teaspoon baking powder

For the syrup
juice of 4 oranges
finely grated zest of 2 oranges
juice of 1 lemon
110g/4 oz caster sugar
150ml/5fl oz water

To serve
icing sugar, sifted

290ml/½ pint double cream, lightly whipped

1. Make the cake: boil the oranges in water in a saucepan for about 1 hour or until very soft. Remove from the water and allow to cool. Cut the oranges in half, and remove and discard any pips. Purée the skin and pulp in a food processor or push through a sieve.

2. Chop the almonds finely and toast very lightly under the grill, taking care that they do not burn. Allow to cool.

3. Meanwhile, preheat the oven to 180°C/350°F/gas mark 4. Grease a 23cm/9in springform cake tin and line the base with a disc of greased greaseproof paper.

4. Put the eggs and sugar into a heatproof bowl fitted over (not in) a saucepan of gently simmering water and whisk until thick and pale. (If using an electric beater, no heat is necessary.)

5. Mix together the orange pulp, almonds and baking powder and fold immediately and quickly into the egg and sugar mixture. Pour into the prepared tin.

6. Bake in the centre of the oven for about 1 hour or until firm to the touch.

7. Remove from the oven and allow to cool in the tin for 20 minutes, then loosen carefully and turn out on to a wire rack. Leave to cool completely.

8. Meanwhile, make the syrup: put the orange juice and zest with the lemon juice, sugar and water into a small saucepan and bring slowly to the boil. Reduce the heat and simmer for about 20 minutes until syrupy. Remove from the heat and allow to cool.

9. To serve: dust the top of the cake with icing sugar and serve each piece with some syrup and a spoonful of whipped cream.

NOTE: This cake remains moist for some time but if being kept for more than a week it should be frozen. Otherwise keep it in an airtight container in a cool, dry place.

4 CHOCOLATE CAKES

Any sort of chocolate cake is very popular with most people. The cakes in this chapter vary from having just a touch of chocolate to being very rich and chocolatey indeed. Some are very easy and quick to make, whereas others are more complicated and suitable for special occasions.

Chocolate can sometimes be tricky to work with but by following a few simple rules there should be no problems. When melting chocolate by itself always place it in a bowl set over, and not in, a saucepan of gently simmering water. (Chocolate can also be successfully melted in a microwave.)

If chocolate is allowed to get too hot it will become dull and grainy. If it gets so hot that the oil comes out of the chocolate, it is impossible to use and should be thrown away. If you are melting chocolate with other ingredients, always do this in a heavy-bottomed saucepan.

If liquid is added to melted chocolate it will seize and become very thick. This is very difficult to correct. Quite a lot of hot water added to it will make the chocolate liquid again but will alter the properties of the liquid in the cake.

◆ ◆

Chocolate Brownies

MAKES 12
melted lard or oil for greasing tin
110g/4oz plain chocolate, chopped
110g//4oz butter
225g/8oz caster sugar
2 eggs, beaten
110g/4oz plain flour
½ teaspoon baking powder
110g/4oz chopped walnuts
a pinch of salt

1. Preheat the oven to 180°C/350°F/gas mark 4.
2. Grease a shallow 28 × 18cm/11 × 7in tin.
3. Put the chocolate into a heatproof bowl with the butter. Fit the bowl over (not in) a saucepan of gently simmering water.
4. When the chocolate and butter have melted, remove the bowl from the heat and stir in all the remaining ingredients. Pour the mixture into the prepared tin.
5. Bake in the centre of the oven for 30 minutes or until the centre is firm to the touch. Remove the cake from the oven and allow to cool in the tin for 10 minutes, then cut into 12 squares, transfer to a wire rack and leave to cool completely.

♦ ♦

Triple Chocolate Brownies

MAKES 24
melted lard or oil for greasing tin
110g/4oz butter
200g/7oz plain chocolate, chopped
110g/4oz caster sugar
2 eggs, lightly beaten
225g/8oz plain flour
140g/5oz white chocolate, chopped
85g/3oz milk chocolate, chopped

1. Preheat the oven to 180°C/350°F/gas mark 4. Grease a 20cm/8in square deep cake tin and line the base with a piece of greased greaseproof paper.

2. Melt the butter and dark chocolate in a saucepan over a low heat. Remove from the heat and allow to cool slightly, then stir in the sugar and eggs.
3. Mix together the flour and white and milk chocolates and fold into the plain chocolate mixture. Pour into the prepared tin.
4. Bake in the centre of the oven for 35 minutes or until the centre is firm to the touch.
5. Remove the cake from the oven and allow to cool completely in the tin, then turn out and cut into squares.

NOTE: 85g/3oz chopped pecan nuts can be substituted for the milk chocolate.

♦ ♦

Macadamia Nut Brownies

MAKES ABOUT 16
Macadamia nuts are delicious in this recipe but if you have difficulty in finding them you could use brazil nuts, hazelnuts or almonds instead. The brownies can be kept in the refrigerator for a couple of days.

melted lard or oil for greasing tin
110g/4oz unsalted butter
110g/4oz plain chocolate
2 eggs

170g/6oz caster sugar
55ml/2fl oz dark rum
110g/4oz plain flour
110g/4oz macadamia nuts, chopped

For the icing
110ml/4fl oz double cream
1 tablespoon dark rum
110g/4oz plain chocolate

1. Preheat the oven to 180°C/350°F/gas mark 4. Grease a 20cm/8in shallow square tin and line with a piece of greased greaseproof paper.
2. Melt the butter and chocolate in a

saucepan over a low heat without allowing to get too hot. Remove and allow to cool.

3. Beat the eggs and sugar together until light and thick. Stir in the cooled chocolate mixture and the rum.

4. Sift the flour and add to the mixture with the macadamia nuts. Fold in carefully and thoroughly, using a large metal spoon.

5. Bake in the centre of the oven for 30 minutes or until the centre is firm to the touch.

6. Remove the cake from the oven and allow to cool completely in the tin, then turn out on to a wire rack.

7. Meanwhile, make the icing: put the cream into a saucepan and bring to the boil. Remove from the heat and add the rum and chocolate. Stir until the chocolate melts. Allow to cool until the icing thickens.

8. When the cake is cold, spread the icing over the top and place in the refrigerator to set. Cut into small squares to serve.

♦ ♦

All-in-one Chocolate Cake

melted lard or oil for greasing tin
85g/3oz self-raising flour
a pinch of salt
30g/1oz cocoa powder
2 eggs
110g/4oz caster sugar
110g/4oz butter, softened
2–3 drops of vanilla essence
2–3 tablespoons warm water
soured cream and chocolate icing (see page 143)

1. Preheat the oven to 180°C/350°F/gas mark 4. Grease a 18cm/7in deep cake tin and line with a disc of greased greaseproof paper.

2. Sift together the flour, salt and cocoa powder into a mixing bowl.

3. Add the eggs, sugar, butter and vanilla essence. Beat with an electric beater for 2 minutes. Add the warm water and beat for 1 further minute. Pour into the prepared tin.

4. Bake in the centre of the oven for 25–30 minutes or until the top springs back when pressed lightly with a fingertip.

5. Remove the cake from the oven and allow to cool in the tin for 10 minutes, then turn out on to a wire rack and leave to cool completely.

6. When the cake is cold, split in half horizontally and sandwich together with half of the icing. Spread the remaining icing on top of the cake. Allow to set.

♦ ♦

Chocolate Fudge Cake

melted lard or oil for greasing tin
110g/4oz butter
110g/4oz caster sugar
2 eggs, beaten
110g/4oz self-raising flour
2 tablespoons golden syrup
30g/1oz ground almonds
a pinch of salt
30g/1oz cocoa powder

For the icing
110g/4oz granulated sugar
110ml/4fl oz milk
140g/5oz plain chocolate, chopped
55g/2oz butter
2 tablespoons double cream
2 teaspoons vanilla essence

1. Preheat the oven to 180°C/350°F/gas mark 4. Grease a 10cm/7in deep cake tin and line the base with a disc of greased greaseproof paper.
2. Cream the butter in a mixing bowl until soft. Add the sugar and beat until light and fluffy.
3. Add the eggs gradually to the creamed mixture, beating well after each addition. Beat in 1 teaspoon of the flour if necessary, to prevent the mixture from curdling.
4. Stir in the syrup and ground almonds. Sift together the flour, salt and cocoa powder and fold into the mixture, using a large metal spoon, to achieve a reluctant dropping consistency. If it is too stiff, add a little water or milk. Turn into the prepared tin and spread out evenly.
5. Bake in the centre of the oven for 40 minutes or until the cake is well risen and feels spongy to the touch. Turn out on to a wire rack and leave to cool.
6. Meanwhile, make the icing: put the sugar and milk into a saucepan over a low heat. Allow the sugar to dissolve, then bring up to the boil. Simmer, without stirring, for 8 minutes.
7. Remove the pan from the heat and stir in the chocolate; add the butter, cream and vanilla essence. Stir until completely melted. Put into a bowl, cover and chill for 2 hours until the icing is spreadable.
8. When the cake is cold, split in half horizontally and sandwich together with one-quarter of the icing. Spread the remaining icing on the top and sides of the cake, swirling it to give a frosted appearance. Allow to set.

◆ ◆

Devil's Food Cake

This sticky, rich chocolate cake can be served plain, or the centre can be filled with whipped cream and/or fruit.

melted lard or oil for greasing tin
225g/8oz caster sugar
55g/2oz cocoa powder
220ml/8fl oz buttermilk
110g/4oz plain flour
1 teaspoon baking powder
a pinch of salt
55g/2oz butter
1 egg, beaten
½ teaspoon vanilla essence

For the filling (optional)
150ml/5fl oz double cream, whipped

1. Preheat the oven to 180°C/350°F/gas mark 4. Grease a 1.25 litre/2 pint ring mould very well (preferably with lard).
2. Mix together 110g/4oz of the sugar, the cocoa powder and 75ml/3fl oz of the buttermilk in a bowl. Leave to stand for 10 minutes.
3. Sift together the flour, baking powder and salt.
4. Cream the butter and the remaining sugar in a mixing bowl until light and fluffy. Gradually add the egg, beating well after each addition.
5. Fold in the flour mixture carefully, using a large metal spoon, and mix in the remaining buttermilk and the vanilla essence. Finally, fold in the cocoa mixture. Pour into the prepared ring mould.
6. Bake in the centre of the oven for 30 minutes or until firm to the touch.
7. Remove the cake from the oven and allow to cool in the ring mould for 5 minutes, then turn out on to a wire rack and leave to cool completely.
8. Serve with whipped cream in the centre, if liked.

NOTE: This cake can be frozen very successfully without the cream.

◆ ◆

Very Rich Chocolate Cake

This recipe is an adaptation of a cake created by the American cookery writer Martha Stewart. It should be very moist and soft in the centre. If it is overbaked it becomes very dry. It is good as a birthday cake or as a pudding.

For the cake
melted lard or oil for greasing tin
55g/2oz sultanas, chopped
55ml/2fl oz brandy
3 eggs
140g/5oz caster sugar
200g/7oz plain chocolate, chopped
2 tablespoons water
110g/4oz unsalted butter
55g/2oz plain flour, sifted
85g/3oz ground almonds

For the icing
140g/5oz plain chocolate, cut into small pieces
150ml/5fl oz double cream

1. Soak the sultanas in the brandy overnight.
2. Preheat the oven to 180°C/350°F/gas mark 4. Grease a moule-à-manqué or 20cm/8in cake tin. Line the base with a disc of greased greaseproof paper.
3. Separate the eggs. Beat the egg yolks and sugar until pale and mousse-like.
4. Put the chocolate and water into a heatproof bowl fitted over (not in) a saucepan of simmering water. Stir until melted, then stir in the butter piece by piece until the mixture is smooth. Allow to cool slightly, then stir into the egg yolk mixture.
5. Fold the flour carefully into the egg yolk and chocolate mixture with the ground almonds, sultanas and brandy, using a large metal spoon.
6. Whisk the egg whites until stiff but not dry and fold into the chocolate mixture. Turn into the prepared tin.
7. Bake in the centre of the oven for 35–40 minutes (the centre should still be moist).
8. Remove the cake from the oven and allow to cool completely in the tin, then turn out on to a wire rack.
9. Make the icing: heat the chocolate and cream in a small saucepan. Stir until all the chocolate has melted and the mixture is smooth. Allow to cool and thicken to a coating consistency.
10. When the cake is cold, pour over the icing and allow to set for at least 2 hours.

◆ ◆

Chocolate Genoise

melted lard or oil for greasing tin
4 eggs
110g/4oz caster sugar
55g/2oz unsalted butter, melted and cooled
85g/3oz plain flour, sifted
30g/1oz cocoa powder, sifted

1. Preheat the oven to 190°C/375°F/gas mark 5. Grease a 20cm/8in moule-à-manqué tin and line the base with a disc of greased greaseproof paper. Dust with caster sugar and then flour. Tap out any excess.
2. Place the eggs and sugar in a large heatproof bowl and fit over (not in) a saucepan of gently simmering water. Whisk until the mixture is light, thick and fluffy. (If using an electric beater, no heat is required.)
3. Remove the bowl from the heat and continue whisking until the mixture is cool and a ribbon trail is left when the whisk is lifted. Do not over-whisk, and stop if the mixture begins to lose bulk. Fold in the butter quickly. If you work slowly the cake will collapse.
4. Sift the flour and cocoa powder together on to the mixture and fold in, using a large metal spoon. Turn into the prepared tin and tap it lightly on the work surface to get rid of any large air pockets.
5. Bake in the centre of the oven for 25–35 minutes or until the top springs back when pressed lightly with a fingertip.
6. Remove the cake from the oven and allow to cool in the tin for 2 minutes, then turn out on to a wire rack and leave to cool completely.

Tiramisu Cake

This cake is based on a classic genoise recipe (see page 35). As this can prove a difficult cake to master, a small amount of baking powder is added to ensure a good result! Tiramisu makes a wonderful rich dinner-party dessert.

oil for greasing tin
4 large eggs
125g/4½oz caster sugar
2 teaspoons instant coffee, dissolved in hot water
55g/2oz butter, melted and cooled
100g/3½oz plain flour
½ teaspoon baking powder

For the syrup
30g/1oz granulated sugar
5 tablespoons water
1 tablespoon Marsala

For the filling
2 teaspoons Marsala
250g/9oz mascarpone or cream cheese
2 teaspoons icing sugar

For dusting
cocoa powder

1. Preheat the oven to 180°C/350°F/gas mark 4.
2. Oil a 20cm/8in moule-à-manqué tin or round cake tin and line the base with a disc of oiled greaseproof paper. Dust first with caster sugar and then with flour. Tap out the excess.
3. Break the eggs into a heatproof bowl, add the sugar and fit the bowl over (not in) a saucepan of gently simmering water. Whisk until the mixture has doubled in bulk. Remove from the heat, add the coffee and continue whisking, off the heat, until the mixture has cooled. (If using an electric beater, no heat is required.)
4. Using a large metal spoon, quickly fold in the butter and the flour sifted with the baking powder. If you work too slowly the cake will collapse. Turn into the prepared tin and spread out evenly.
5. Bake in the centre of the oven for about 30–35 minutes or until the top springs back when pressed lightly with a fingertip.
6. Remove from the oven and allow to cool slightly in the tin, then turn out on to a wire rack and leave to cool completely.
7. Make the syrup: put the sugar and water into a heavy saucepan and stir over a low heat without boiling until the sugar has dissolved completely. Bring to the boil and boil until syrupy. Remove from the heat, allow to cool slightly and add the Marsala.
8. When the cake is cold, split it in half horizontally, brush with half the syrup and leave on a wire rack to get cold.
9. Mix together the filling ingredients and spread on the bottom layer of the cake. Sift over a thin layer of cocoa powder and cover with the top layer of the cake. Brush with the remaining syrup.
10. Just before serving, dust with sifted cocoa powder.

◆◆◆◆◆◆◆◆◆◆◆◆◆◆◆◆◆◆◆◆◆◆

Chocolate Yoghurt Cake

This is an adaptation of a recipe given to me by Rosemary Gaskell Taylor who attended a holiday course at Leith's School of Food & Wine. It improves with keeping and is excellent for children's birthday cakes as it is very easy to cut into shapes.

melted lard or oil for greasing tin
3 eggs
150ml/5fl oz sunflower oil
150ml/5fl oz natural yoghurt
4 tablespoons golden syrup
85g/3oz caster sugar
225g/8oz self-raising flour
4 tablespoons cocoa powder
½ teaspoon bicarbonate of soda

1. Preheat the oven to 170°C/325°F/gas mark 3. Grease a 20cm/8in deep cake tin and line the base with a disc of greased greaseproof paper.
2. Beat together the eggs, oil, yoghurt, syrup and sugar in a mixing bowl.
3. Sift together the flour, cocoa powder and bicarbonate of soda and fold into the egg mixture, using a large metal spoon. Pour into the prepared tin.
4. Bake in the centre of the oven for about 1¼–1½ hours or until the top springs back when pressed lightly with a fingertip.
5. Remove the cake from the oven and allow to cool in the tin for 10 minutes, then turn out on to a wire rack and leave to cool completely.

NOTE: This cake can also be baked in a roasting tin measuring approximately 25 × 20cm/10 × 8in. It will then take only 45–60 minutes to bake.

◆◆◆◆◆◆◆◆◆◆◆◆◆◆◆◆◆◆◆◆◆◆

Orange and Almond Gâteau with Chocolate Ganache

For the gâteau
melted lard or oil for greasing tin
4 eggs
110g/4oz caster sugar, plus 1 extra teaspoon
grated zest of 2 oranges
55g/2oz plain flour
½ teaspoon baking powder
110g/4oz ground almonds

For the ganache
110ml/4fl oz double cream
170g/6oz plain chocolate, cut into small pieces

For the orange syrup
30g/1oz sugar
55ml/2fl oz water
juice of 1 orange

To finish
icing sugar, sifted

1. Preheat the oven to 170°C/350°F/gas mark 4. Grease a 20cm/8in moule-à-manqué tin and line the base with a disc of greased greaseproof paper.

2. Separate the eggs and put the yolks and 110g/4oz sugar into a bowl. Whisk, preferably with an electric beater, until light and creamy. Fold in the orange zest.

3. Whisk the egg whites until stiff. Whisk in the extra teaspoon of sugar. Fold carefully into the egg yolk mixture, using a large metal spoon.

4. Sift the flour with the baking powder, mix with the ground almonds and fold very carefully and quickly into the cake mixture. Pour into the prepared tin.

5. Bake in the centre of the oven for 35–40 minutes or until the sides have shrunk away from the tin very slightly and the top springs back when pressed lightly with a fingertip. Resist the temptation to open the oven door before 30 minutes have passed as the cake could collapse.

6. Remove the cake from the oven and allow to cool in the tin for 5 minutes, then turn out on to a wire rack and leave to cool completely.

7. Meanwhile, make the ganache: bring the cream to boiling point in a saucepan. Remove from the heat and stir in the chocolate. Allow the mixture to stand for 2 minutes, then beat until smooth. Set aside to cool at room temperature. Do not refrigerate.

8. Make the orange syrup: put the sugar and water into a small saucepan and heat gently until the sugar has dissolved completely, then bring to the boil. Boil for 1 minute, then remove from the heat and allow to cool. Stir the orange juice into the cooled syrup.

9. When the cake is cold, beat the chocolate ganache with an electric whisk for 2 minutes or until it has lightened in colour and texture.

10. Split the cake in half horizontally. Brush the bottom layer of the cake with half the orange syrup. Spread over a little of the whipped ganache. Cover with the top layer of cake and brush with the remaining syrup.

11. Spread the top and sides of the cake with the remaining ganache, as neatly as possible. Chill in the refrigerator for 30 minutes.

12. Serve dusted with a little icing sugar.

♦ ♦

Chocolate and Orange Cake

This is a moist chocolate gâteau. As it is filled with cream it can be served at teatime or as a very rich pudding.

melted lard or oil for greasing tin
85g/3oz plain chocolate, chopped
340g/12oz soft light brown sugar
110g/4oz butter
grated zest of 1 orange
225g/8oz plain flour
2 eggs, beaten
1 teaspoon bicarbonate of soda
290ml/½ pint milk, warmed

For the filling
290ml/½ pint double cream, whipped
2 tablespoons icing sugar
grated zest of 1 orange

For the icing
110g/4oz plain chocolate
4 tablespoons milk

1. Preheat the oven to 180°C/350°F/gas mark 4. Grease a 20cm/8in deep cake tin and line with a disc of greased greaseproof paper.
2. Put the chocolate, sugar and butter into a small saucepan and melt over a gentle heat, stirring until quite smooth. Remove from the heat, add the orange zest and allow to cool.
3. Sift the flour into a mixing bowl. Make a well in the centre and add the eggs and melted chocolate mixture. Add the bicarbonate of soda to the milk and add to the well. Mix carefully, gradually

incorporating the flour, and beat to a thick, smooth batter. Pour into the prepared tin.
4. Bake in the centre of the oven for about 1 hour or until the sides have shrunk away from the tin slightly and the top springs back when pressed lightly with a fingertip.
5. Remove the cake from the oven and allow to cool in the tin for 20 minutes, then turn out on to a wire rack and leave to cool completely.
6. Make the filling: mix the cream with the sugar and orange zest.
7. Make the icing: put the chocolate and milk into a saucepan and melt over a gentle heat until smooth. Remove from the heat and allow to cool to a thick coating consistency.
8. When the cake is cold, split horizontally into three, very carefully. Sandwich the layers together with the cream. Pour the chocolate icing evenly over the top. Allow to set.

♦ ♦

Chocolate Polenta Cake

This delicious cake can also be served as a pudding and is perfect with fresh raspberries and Greek yoghurt or crème fraîche.

melted lard or oil for greasing tin
225g/8oz plain chocolate, chopped
110g/4oz unsalted butter
5 eggs
140g/5oz caster sugar
3 tablespoons dark rum

85g/3oz fine polenta

1. Preheat the oven to 180°C/350°F/gas mark 4. Grease a 20cm/8in moule-à-manqué tin or a 22cm/9in sandwich tin. Line the base with a disc of greased greaseproof paper. Dust lightly with caster sugar and then flour. Tap out the excess.
2. Put the chocolate into a saucepan with the butter. Melt gently over a low heat. Remove from the heat and allow to cool slightly in a bowl.
3. Separate the eggs. Beat the yolks with 85g/3oz of the sugar. Add 1 tablespoon of

the rum and continue beating until thick and pale.

4. Fold the melted chocolate mixture into the egg and sugar mixture.

5. Whisk the egg whites until thick and holding a medium peak. Gradually whisk in the remaining sugar until thick and glossy.

6. Fold the remaining rum and the polenta into the chocolate mixture, using a large metal spoon, and finally fold in the egg whites. Pour into the prepared tin.

7. Bake in the centre of the oven for 40–50 minutes or until a sharp knife or skewer inserted into the centre comes out clean.

8. Remove the cake from the oven and allow to cool in the tin for 10 minutes, then turn out on to a serving plate and leave to cool completely.

NOTE: The cake is turned directly on to a plate as it is fragile and can break if it is moved.

♦ ♦

Mocha Loaf

This recipe uses cooked, sieved potato which gives the cake a moist, close texture.

melted lard or oil for greasing tin
55g/2oz plain chocolate, chopped
2 teaspoons instant coffee
3 tablespoons milk
170g/6oz butter
170g/6oz caster sugar
110g/4oz boiled potatoes, sieved and cooled
3 large eggs, beaten
170g/6oz self-raising flour
55g/2oz cocoa powder
1 teaspoon baking powder

For the icing
170g/6oz plain chocolate, chopped
30g/1oz butter
2 tablespoons water

1. Preheat the oven to 180°C/350°F/gas mark 4. Grease a 900g/2lb loaf tin and line the base with a piece of greased greaseproof paper.

2. Put the chocolate into a heatproof bowl with the coffee and milk. Fit the bowl over (not in) a saucepan of gently simmering water and melt the chocolate. Do not allow it to get too hot. Remove from the heat and allow to cool slightly.

3. Cream the butter and the sugar together in a mixing bowl until light and fluffy. Mix in the potato. Add the eggs gradually with the cooled, but still runny, chocolate mixture, beating well after each addition.

4. Sift the flour, cocoa and baking powder together on to the mixture and fold in carefully, using a large metal spoon. Turn into the prepared tin.

5. Bake in the centre of the oven for 30–40 minutes or until the top springs back when pressed lightly with a fingertip.

6. Remove the cake from the oven and allow to cool in the tin for a few minutes, then turn out on to a wire rack and leave to cool completely.

7. Make the icing: put the chocolate into a heatproof bowl with the butter and water. Fit over (not in) a saucepan of gently simmering water and melt the chocolate, stirring occasionally. Remove from the heat and allow the icing to cool until it will coat

the back of a spoon.

8. When the cake is cold, spread the icing over the top and allow to set.

NOTE: This cake freezes well and will become a little moister after a couple of days if kept in an airtight tin.

◆ ◆

Sachertorte

This rich chocolate cake originates from Vienna. It's a speciality of the Sacher Hotel and is said to have been invented by Franz Sacher in the mid-1800s. The true recipe is a closely guarded secret but this one is a close approximation. It is perfect for a birthday cake, or you can finish it off traditionally by piping 'Sacher' in chocolate across the top.

melted lard or oil for greasing tin
170g/6oz plain chocolate, chopped
140g/5oz butter, softened
110g/4oz icing sugar, sifted
6 eggs
110g/4oz caster sugar
125g/4½oz plain flour, sifted

For the glaze
225g/8oz apricot jam
½ teaspoon lemon juice

For the icing
285g/10oz granulated sugar
290ml/½ pint water
225g/8oz plain chocolate, cut into small pieces

1. Preheat the oven to 180°C/350°F/gas mark 4. Grease a 22cm/9in springform tin and line the base with a disc of greased greaseproof paper.

2. Melt the chocolate in a heatproof bowl fitted over (not in) a saucepan of gently simmering water. Remove from the heat and allow to cool slightly.

3. Cream the butter in a mixing bowl, add the icing sugar and beat well until pale and fluffy. Separate the eggs and add the yolks one at a time, beating well after each addition.

4. Whisk the egg whites until stiff. Whisk in the caster sugar gradually and whisk again until stiff and shiny.

5. Working quite quickly but carefully, mix the cooled melted chocolate into the creamed mixture, then fold in the egg whites and flour, using a large metal spoon. Pour into the prepared tin.

6. Bake in the centre of the oven for 50 minutes or until a sharp knife or skewer inserted into the centre comes out clean.

7. Remove the cake from the oven and allow to cool in the tin for 10 minutes, then loosen, turn out on to a wire rack and leave to cool completely.

8. Meanwhile, make the glaze: heat the apricot jam with the lemon juice in a saucepan. Bring up to the boil, then push through a sieve and allow to cool slightly. It should be warm when it is used.

9. Make the icing: put the granulated sugar into a thick-bottomed saucepan and add the water. Heat very gently, ensuring that the sugar dissolves before the water boils. Once the sugar has dissolved, bring up to the boil

and boil to the thread stage (when a little syrup is placed between a wet finger and thumb and the fingers are opened, it should form a sticky thread about 2.5cm/1in long). The temperature will be approximately 105°C/225°F.

10. Remove the sugar syrup from the heat and place the pan in a roasting tin filled with warm water. This will prevent the syrup from cooking further. Leave for 1 minute, then add the chocolate and stir constantly until the chocolate has melted and the icing has cooled and achieved a coating consistency.

11. When the cake is cold, place upside-down on a wire rack set over a tray. Paint the top and sides with the warm apricot glaze and allow to cool. Pour the icing quickly over the cake, tilting it as the icing runs over it, to ensure a smooth, even covering. Do not disturb the icing once it is on the cake. Allow to set.

◆ ◆

Le Gascon

This is a complicated recipe but the end result justifies all the effort. It is a good alternative to a birthday cake if you want to serve it as a pudding. It can be made the day before and it also freezes very well.

SERVES 8–10

3-egg quantity sponge fingers (see page 4)
3-egg quantity chocolate genoise (see page 80)
2 tablespoons Armagnac or brandy
150ml/5fl oz sugar syrup (see page 143)
3-egg yolk quantity rich chocolate mousse (see page 88)
2-egg white quantity prune mousse (see page 88)
110g/4oz chocolate quantity glaçage koba (see page 143)

1. Trim one end of the sponge fingers and use to line the sides of a 20cm/8in springform tin, trimming if necessary to make sure all the fingers are the same height.

2. Split the chocolate genoise in half horizontally and place one half cut side up in the bottom of the tin.

3. Add the Armagnac to the sugar syrup. Brush both cakes with the syrup.

4. Pour the chocolate mousse into the tin until it comes halfway up the sponge fingers. Allow to set.

5. Place the other half of the genoise cut-side up on top of the set chocolate mousse and brush with the syrup.

6. Pour over the prune mousse, leaving a 5mm/¼in space at the top. Allow to set.

7. To serve, unclip the tin and carefully ease the cake out on to a serving plate.

◆ ◆

Rich Chocolate Mousse

70g/2½oz granulated sugar
110ml/4fl oz water
3 egg yolks
170g/6oz plain chocolate, chopped
340ml/12fl oz double cream, lightly whipped

1. Put the sugar and water into a small saucepan and heat gently until the sugar has dissolved completely, then bring to the boil.
2. Boil to the thread stage (when a little syrup is placed between a wet finger and thumb and the fingers are opened, it should form a sticky thread about 2.5cm/1in long). Allow to cool slightly.
3. Pour the sugar syrup over the egg yolks, whisking all the time. Continue whisking until the mixture is thick and mousse-like.
4. Melt the chocolate carefully in a heatproof bowl fitted over (not in) a saucepan of gently simmering water. Fold the chocolate into the egg mixture, using a large metal spoon.
5. Immediately fold in the cream carefully. Use as required.

♦ ♦

Prune Mousse

110g/4oz pitted prunes
150ml/5fl oz water
30ml/1fl oz Armagnac or brandy
7g/¼oz gelatine
110g/4oz granulated sugar
150ml/5fl oz water
2 egg whites
150ml/5fl oz double cream, lightly whipped

1. Soak the prunes in the water and Armagnac for a day, then purée them in a liquidizer or food processor.
2. Soak the gelatine in 3 tablespoons water.
3. Put the sugar and water into a small saucepan and heat gently until the sugar has dissolved completely, then bring to the boil. Boil to the thread stage (when a little syrup is placed between a wet finger and thumb and the fingers are opened, it should form a sticky thread about 2.5cm/1in long). Leave to cool for 30 seconds.
4. Whisk the egg whites until stiff and gradually add the sugar syrup, whisking all the time until the mixture has formed a thick, shiny meringue.
5. Dissolve the gelatine over a gentle heat without boiling and when clear, runny and warm, add to the prune purée.
6. Whisk the purée gradually into the meringue mixture. Fold in the cream, using a large metal spoon.

♦ ♦

Gâteau Opera

This gâteau is fairly simple to make but does take a long time. It freezes well although it is best to put the chocolate on top once it has defrosted.

For the cake
melted lard or oil for greasing tin
100g/3½oz caster sugar
3 eggs
3 egg whites
100g/3½oz ground almonds
30g/1oz plain flour
a pinch of baking powder
30g/1oz unsalted butter, melted and cooled

For the buttercream
55g/2oz granulated sugar
100ml/3½fl oz water
2 egg yolks
3 teaspoons instant coffee
1 tablespoon boiling water
70g/2½oz unsalted butter, softened
70g/2½oz salted butter, softened

For the ganache
70g/6oz plain chocolate, chopped
85ml/3fl oz milk
170ml/6fl oz double cream

For the coffee syrup
100g/3½oz granulated sugar
100ml/3½fl oz water
1 teaspoon instant coffee

For the top
140g/5oz plain chocolate, chopped

1. Make the cake: preheat the oven to 200°C/400°F/gas mark 6. Grease a 20cm/ 8in square cake tin and line the base with a piece of greased greaseproof paper.
2. Put 85g/3oz of the sugar and the 3 eggs into a large bowl and beat with an electric whisk until the mixture is light and holds a trail when the whisk is removed from the mixture.
3. Whisk the egg whites until stiff and whisk in the remaining sugar. Fold carefully into the egg and sugar mixture, using a large metal spoon.
4. Mix together the ground almonds, flour and baking powder. Fold the butter and the flour mixture into the cake mixture, using a large metal spoon and being careful not to overfold. Pour into the prepared tin.
5. Bake in the oven for about 15 minutes or until just firm to the touch. Turn on to a wire rack and leave to cool.
6. When the cake is cold, remove the lining paper and very carefully split the cake horizontally into 3 layers.
7. Make the buttercream: dissolve the sugar in the water in a saucepan, then bring to the boil. Boil to the thread stage (when a little syrup is placed between a wet finger and thumb and the fingers are opened, it should form a sticky thread about 2.5cm/1in long).
8. Whisk the egg yolks and pour on the hot sugar syrup. Continue whisking until thick.
9. Dissolve the coffee in the water. Whisk the butters gradually into the egg mixture with the coffee.
10. Make the chocolate ganache: put the chocolate into a heatproof bowl and melt over (not in) a saucepan of gently simmering water.
11. Bring the milk to the boil and add to the melted chocolate. Remove from the heat and allow to cool, stirring occasionally. Whip the cream until it thickens slightly. Fold it into the chocolate mixture.

12. Make the coffee syrup: put the sugar and water into a small saucepan and heat gently until the sugar has dissolved completely, then bring to the boil. Boil for 2 minutes, then add the coffee. Remove from the heat and allow to cool.

13. Assemble the cake: brush the bottom layer with about one-third of the coffee syrup and spread with all the buttercream. Place the middle layer carefully on top, brush with more syrup and spread with two-thirds of the chocolate ganache. Place the top layer on top, brush with the remaining syrup and spread with the remaining ganache in a thin layer. Smooth very well and chill.

14. Put the chocolate for the top into a heatproof bowl and melt over (not in) a saucepan of gently simmering water. Reserving a little for piping, spread the remainder very carefully over the top of the chilled cake, as smoothly as you can.

15. Pipe the word 'opera' on top with the remaining melted chocolate.

♦ ♦

Chocolate Rose Leaf Gâteau

This is a relatively simple gâteau to make but the chocolate rose leaves need to be made in advance. The cake keeps moist for several days, or it can be frozen completely assembled, although the chocolate leaves may develop a little bit of white bloom.

For the cake
melted lard or oil for greasing tin
110g/4oz plain chocolate, chopped
2 tablespoons water
110g/4oz butter
140g/5oz caster sugar
3 eggs
55g/2oz ground almonds
70g/2½oz fresh white breadcrumbs
2 teaspoons vanilla essence

For the icing
110g/4oz plain chocolate, chopped

3 tablespoons strong coffee
15g/½oz butter
a few drops of vanilla essence

chocolate rose leaves, using 170g/6oz plain chocolate (see page 91)

To finish
icing sugar, sifted

1. Preheat the oven to 190°C/375°F/gas mark 5. Grease a 20cm/8in moule-à-manqué tin and line with a disc of greased greaseproof paper.

2. Put the chocolate and water into a small heatproof bowl and melt over (not in) a saucepan of gently simmering water.

3. Meanwhile, cream the butter well in a mixing bowl, add the sugar and beat well until light and creamy. Separate the eggs and add the yolks one at a time, beating well after each addition.

4. Stir in the ground almonds, breadcrumbs, vanilla essence and melted chocolate to make a fairly stiff texture.

5. Whisk the egg whites until they form soft to medium peaks and stir 1 tablespoon into the cake mixture, to loosen it. Fold in the remaining egg whites carefully, using a large metal spoon. Pour into the prepared tin.

6. Bake in the centre of the oven for 30 minutes, then turn the temperature down to 180°C/350°F/gas mark 4 and cover the top of the cake with a piece of greaseproof paper. Bake for 15–20 further minutes or until the top springs back when pressed lightly with a fingertip.

7. Remove the cake from the oven and allow to cool in the tin for 10 minutes, then turn out on to a wire rack and leave to cool completely.

8. Meanwhile, make the icing: put the chocolate, coffee, butter and vanilla essence into a heatproof bowl and place over (not in) a saucepan of gently simmering water. Stir until it has melted, and do not allow it to get too hot. Remove the bowl from the pan and leave to cool to a coating consistency, stirring occasionally.

9. When the cake is cold, spread the icing over the top and sides. Arrange the chocolate rose leaves carefully, overlapping in a circular pattern, and dust lightly with icing sugar.

◆ ◆

Chocolate Rose Leaves

These make a lovely decoration for a special cake or gâteau. This quantity will make 30–40 leaves depending on the size. Make them in advance and store them carefully in a sealed container, in a cool place.

170g/6oz plain chocolate
30–40 rose leaves, well washed and dried

1. Chop the chocolate into small pieces and place in a heatproof bowl over (not in) a saucepan of gently simmering water. Stir occasionally until the chocolate has melted. Do not allow it to get too hot as this will make the chocolate dull and could give it a white bloom once it has set.

2. Coat the veined underside of each rose leaf carefully, either painting the chocolate on with a pastry brush or dipping the leaf into the chocolate. Place the leaves, chocolate side up, on a wire rack and leave to set. If the room is hot it would be advisable to put them in the refrigerator to set.

3. Once the chocolate has set, peel off the leaves carefully. Put the chocolate leaves back into the refrigerator until ready to use.

5 CAKES WITH NUTS

If you wish to vary the flavour of the cakes in this chapter, you can substitute one kind of nut for another. For example, using hazelnuts instead of walnuts in the Apricot and Walnut Loaf will considerably change the flavour but the method and timing will be exactly the same. This could be very useful if you were convinced you had a packet of hazelnuts in your store cupboard but they turned out to be almonds. Always use unsalted nuts.

♦ ♦

Almond Cake

melted lard or oil for greasing tin
140g/5oz butter
140g/5oz caster sugar
finely grated zest of 1 lemon
6 eggs
85g/3oz plain flour
½ teaspoon baking powder
225g/8oz blanched almonds, roughly chopped
1 tablespoon water

1. Preheat the oven to 190°C/375°F/gas mark 5. Grease a 20cm/8in moule-à-manqué tin and line the base with a disc of greased greaseproof paper.
2. Cream the butter and sugar together in a large mixing bowl until light and fluffy. Add the lemon zest. Separate the eggs and beat in the yolks.
3. Sift the flour with the baking powder. Mix with the chopped almonds.
4. Whisk the egg whites until stiff and fold them into the creamed mixture together with the flour and nut mixture and water, using a large metal spoon. Pour into the prepared tin.
5. Bake in the centre of the preheated oven for about 35–40 minutes or until the sides have shrunk away from the sides of the tin slightly and the top springs back when pressed lightly with a fingertip.
6. Remove from the oven and allow to cool in the tin for a few minutes, then turn out on to a wire rack and leave to cool completely.

♦ ♦

Pain de Genes (Rich Almond Cake)

This is delicious served in small pieces with strong coffee after a meal.

melted lard or oil for greasing tin
110g/4oz blanched almonds
3 eggs
140g/5oz caster sugar
55g/2oz potato starch or plain flour
½ teaspoon baking powder
a good pinch of salt
85g/3oz butter
1 tablespoon Amaretto or Kirsch

To finish
icing sugar, sifted

1. Preheat the oven to 180°C/350°F/gas mark 4. Brush a moule-à-manqué or 20cm/8in cake tin with melted butter, line the base with a disc of greaseproof paper and brush again with melted butter.
2. Grind the almonds, but not finely.
3. Whisk the eggs and sugar together until light and fluffy.
4. Sift the flour, baking powder and salt together into a mixing bowl. Stir in the ground almonds. Add to the egg and sugar mixture and half fold in, using a large metal spoon.
5. Melt the butter until runny but not hot and carefully fold it into the cake mixture with the minimum of stirring. Add the Amaretto or Kirsch. Turn the mixture into the prepared tin.
6. Bake in the centre of the oven for 30–35 minutes or until the cake is brown on top and springs back when pressed lightly with a fingertip.
7. Remove the cake from the oven and allow to cool in the tin for 5 minutes, then loosen the sides with a knife and turn out on to a wire rack and leave to cool completely.
8. Serve dusted with icing sugar.

◆ ◆

Mandel Cake

This is a lovely summer cake and can be served as a pudding filled with fresh cream and summer berries.

melted lard or oil for greasing tins
6 eggs
225g/8oz caster sugar
2 tablespoons lemon juice
1 teaspoon finely grated lemon zest
1 teaspoon ground cinnamon

225g/8oz almonds, toasted, cooled and finely
  ground
55g/2oz plain flour
½ teaspoon cream of tartar

For the filling
100ml/3½fl oz double cream
2 tablespoons lemon curd (see page 154)

To finish
icing sugar, sifted

1. Preheat the oven to 180°C/350°F/gas mark 4. Line the base and sides of two 20cm/8in sandwich tins carefully with kitchen foil and grease them.

2. Separate the eggs. Beat the yolks well with half the sugar until pale and fluffy. Gradually beat in the lemon juice and zest and cinnamon.

3. Mix together the almonds and flour.

4. Whisk the egg whites until stiff. Add the cream of tartar and 2 tablespoons of the remaining sugar. Whisk well until stiff and shiny. Gradually add the remaining sugar, whisking well after each addition.

5. Using a large metal spoon, fold the egg whites quickly into the yolk mixture, then fold in the almonds and flour. Do not overmix or the cake will collapse. Divide between the prepared tins and spread out evenly.

6. Bake for 40 minutes or until the tops spring back when pressed lightly with a fingertip.

7. Remove from the oven and allow to cool in the tins for 5 minutes, then turn out on to a wire rack, carefully peel off the lining foil and leave to cool completely.

8. Meanwhile, make the filling: whip the cream until it just holds its shape. Fold in the lemon curd.

9. When the cakes are cool, sandwich together with the filling and dust the top with icing sugar.

♦ ♦

Hazelnut and Apricot Cake

This cake is made without eggs and consequently has a fairly dense texture. The apricot purée makes it very moist and it keeps well. Once iced, it must be kept in the refrigerator.

For the cake
melted lard or oil for greasing tin
55g/2oz dried apricots
290ml/½ pint water
juice of ½ lemon
110g/4oz butter
170g/6oz caster sugar
225g/8oz plain flour
1 teaspoon ground mixed spice

1 teaspoon bicarbonate of soda
110g/4oz toasted hazelnuts, roughly chopped

For the icing
140g/5oz cream cheese
30g/1oz sugar
30g/1oz dried apricots, finely chopped

1. Preheat the oven to 180°C/350°F/gas mark 4. Grease an 18cm/7in cake tin and line the base with a disc of greased greaseproof paper.

2. Put the apricots and water into a saucepan and bring to the boil. Reduce the heat, then simmer gently for 20 minutes or until the apricots are soft.

3. Purée the apricots with the cooking liquid in a food processor or liquidizer, or push it through a sieve. Add the lemon juice and make up to 150ml/5fl oz with water.

4. Meanwhile, cream the butter in a mixing bowl until soft, then add the sugar. Beat together until soft and creamy.

5. Sift the flour together with the mixed spice and bicarbonate of soda.

6. Add the apricot purée to the creamed mixture and fold in the flour and chopped nuts. Mix well. Turn into the prepared tin.

7. Bake in the centre of the oven for about 1 hour. Loosen the edges of the cake with a knife, turn out on to a wire rack and leave to cool completely.

8. Meanwhile, mix together the ingredients for the icing. Taste and add more sugar if necessary.

9. When the cake is cold, spread the icing over the top. Keep in the refrigerator until ready to serve.

◆ ◆

Coffee Walnut Cake

melted lard or oil for greasing tins
170g/6oz butter
170g/6oz caster sugar
3 large eggs (size 2), beaten
170g/6oz self-raising flour, sifted
2 tablespoons coffee essence or very strong instant coffee
85g/3oz chopped walnuts
water (optional)

For the butter icing
110g/4oz butter
170g/6oz icing sugar
2 teaspoons coffee essence

For the glacé icing
110g/4oz icing sugar
boiling water
coffee essence

To decorate
walnut halves

1. Preheat the oven to 180°C/350°F/gas mark 4.

2. Lightly grease two 18cm/7in sandwich tins and line each with a disc of greased greaseproof paper.

3. Cream the butter and sugar together in a mixing bowl until light and fluffy. Beat the eggs gradually into the creamed mixture, a little at a time, beating well after each addition. Add 1 tablespoon of the flour if necessary to prevent the mixture from curdling.

4. Fold in the remaining flour, using a large metal spoon, and add the coffee essence and chopped walnuts. Add some water if necessary to bring the mixture to a dropping consistency. Divide the mixture between the prepared tins and spread out evenly.

5. Bake in the centre of the oven for about 30 minutes or until the cakes are well risen and feel spongy to the fingertips.

6. Remove the cakes to cool in the tins for a few minutes, and then turn out on to a wire rack and leave to cool completely.

7. Meanwhile, make the butter icing: cream the butter in a bowl and add the icing sugar. Beat well and add the coffee essence.

8. Make the glacé icing: sift the icing sugar into a bowl and add a little boiling water and coffee essence to taste. The icing should be of a very thick pouring consistency.

9. When the cakes are cold, sandwich them together with half the butter icing. Pour the glacé icing over the top and decorate with the remaining coffee butter icing, piped into rosettes, and walnut halves.

♦ ♦

Apricot and Walnut Loaf

225g/8oz dried apricots, roughly chopped
290ml/½ pint water
melted lard or oil for greasing tin
225g/8oz caster sugar
85g/3oz butter, melted and cooked
1 egg, beaten
55ml/2fl oz water
110ml/4fl oz orange juice
285g/10oz plain flour, sifted
2 teaspoons baking powder
a pinch of salt
85g/3oz walnuts, chopped

1. Soak the apricots in the water for 30 minutes.

2. Preheat the oven to 180°C/350°F/gas mark 4. Grease a 900g/2lb loaf tin and line the base with a piece of greased greaseproof paper.
3. Mix the sugar, butter, egg, water and orange juice together in a mixing bowl.
4. Sift together the flour, baking powder and salt and add to the sugar and egg mixture. Mix well. Stir in the drained apricots and the walnuts. Pour into the prepared tin.
5. Bake in the centre of the oven for 1–1¼ hours or until a sharp knife or skewer inserted into the centre of the cake comes out clean.
6. Remove from the oven and leave to cool in the tin for 10 minutes, then turn out on to a wire rack and leave to cool completely.

♦ ♦

Lemon Nut Bread

melted lard or oil for greasing tins
450g/1lb butter
450g/1lb caster sugar
6 eggs, beaten
450g/1lb plain flour
1 teaspoon salt
finely grated zest and juice of 3 lemons
225g/8oz raisins
225g/8oz pecan nuts, chopped

1 teaspoon bicarbonate of soda
1 tablespoon water

1. Preheat the oven to 180°C/350°F/gas mark 4. Grease two 900g/2lb loaf tins and line the base of each with a piece of greased greaseproof paper.
2. Cream the butter in a large mixing bowl until soft. Add the sugar and beat until light and fluffy. Add the eggs gradually, beating well after each addition. Add a little of the

Gâteau Opera

Austrian Carrot Cake, Pumpkin Bread, Parsnip and Pecan Cake and Courgette Bread

Coffee and Raisin Cake, Fig and Oat Loaf, Honey Cake and Black Sticky Gingerbread

Fruit Gugelhopf, Panettone and Stollen

Doughnuts and Saffron Cake

Danish Pastries

Drop Scones, Treacle Scones, Singin' Hinny, Apricot Scones,
Sultana Scones and Raspberry Compôte

Raspberry and Blueberry Muffins and Plain Muffins

flour if necessary to prevent the mixture from curdling.

3. Sift the remaining flour with the salt and fold into the mixture, using a large metal spoon. Stir in the lemon zest and juice, raisins and pecan nuts. Mix the bicarbonate of soda with the water and add to the mixture. Turn into the prepared tins.

4. Bake in the oven for 1¼–1½ hours or until the top springs back when pressed lightly with a fingertip.

5. Remove from the oven and allow to cool in the tin for 5 minutes, then turn out on to a wire rack and leave to cool completely.

◆ ◆

Pecan and Rosemary Genoise

oil for greasing tin
4 eggs
125g/4½oz caster sugar
1 teaspoon vanilla essence
125g/4½oz plain flour
85g/3oz pecan nuts, finely chopped
1 teaspoon finely chopped fresh rosemary
55g/2oz butter, melted and cooled

For the filling
4 tablespoons crème fraîche

To finish
icing sugar, sifted

1. Preheat the oven to 190°C/375°F/gas mark 5. Lightly oil a 20cm/8in moule-à-manqué or deep sandwich tin and line the base with a disc of oiled greaseproof paper. Dust first with caster sugar and then with flour. Tap out the excess.

2. Break the eggs into a heatproof bowl, add the sugar and vanilla essence and fit the bowl over (not in) a saucepan of gently simmering water. Whisk until the mixture has doubled in bulk and will leave a ribbon trail on the surface when the whisk is lifted. Remove the bowl from the heat and continue whisking until the mixture has cooled. (If using an electric beater, no heat is necessary.)

3. Sift the flour into the mixture and fold in gently, using a large metal spoon, with the pecan nuts and rosemary. Drizzle the butter around the edge of the bowl and incorporate it just before the nuts and rosemary are completely mixed in.

4. Holding the bowl close to the prepared tin, pour in the mixture, taking care not to lose any bulk.

5. Bake in the centre of the oven for 25–30 minutes or until firm to the touch and the sides have shrunk away from the tin slightly.

6. Remove from the oven and allow to cool in the tin for 5 minutes, then turn out on to a wire rack and leave to cool completely.

7. When the cake is cold, split it in half horizontally and sandwich together with the crème fraîche. Dredge the top with icing sugar.

◆ ◆

Soured Cream and Pecan Cake

melted lard or oil for greasing tin
225g/8oz butter
285g/10oz caster sugar
2 eggs, beaten
285g/10oz self-raising flour, sifted
290ml/½ pint soured cream
2 teaspoons vanilla essence
110g/4oz chopped pecan nuts
1 teaspoon ground cinnamon

1. Preheat the oven to 160°C/325°F/gas mark 3. Grease a 22cm/9in spring clip tin or loose-bottomed tin and line the base with a disc of greased greaseproof paper.
2. Cream the butter in a mixing bowl and add 225g/8oz of the sugar. Beat until soft, pale and creamy. Add the eggs gradually, beating well after each addition. Add a little of the flour if necessary to prevent the mixture from curdling. Fold in the remaining flour and add the soured cream and vanilla essence. Mix well but do not beat.
3. Mix the remaining sugar with the pecan nuts and cinnamon.
4. Put half the cake mixture into the prepared tin. Sprinkle over three-quarters of the pecan mixture. Cover with the remaining cake mixture, spread out evenly and sprinkle over the remaining pecan mixture.
5. Bake in the centre of the oven for 1¼–1½ hours or until a sharp knife or skewer inserted into the centre of the cake comes out clean.
6. Remove from the oven and allow to cool in the tin for 30 minutes, then turn out on to a wire rack and leave to cool completely.

◆ ◆

Streusel Cake

melted lard or oil for greasing tin
225g/8oz butter
225g/8oz caster sugar
3 eggs, beaten
225g/8oz plain flour
1 teaspoon bicarbonate of soda
1 teaspoon baking powder
220ml/8fl oz soured cream

For the streusel mixture
170g/6oz soft light brown sugar
110g/4oz pecan nuts, chopped
30g/1oz plain flour
1½ tablespoons ground cinnamon
55g/2oz butter, melted

1. Preheat the oven to 180°C/350°F/gas mark 4. Grease a 20cm/8in square cake tin and line the base with a piece of greased greaseproof paper.
2. Cream the butter and sugar together in a mixing bowl until light and fluffy. Add the eggs gradually to the creamed mixture, beating well after each addition. Add a little of the flour if necessary to prevent the mixture from curdling.
3. Sift the remaining flour, bicarbonate of soda, and baking powder together and fold into the mixture, using a large metal spoon. Stir in the soured cream.
4. Mix together all the ingredients for the streusel mixture.
5. Spread half the cake mixture in the

bottom of the tin. Sprinkle over half the streusel mixture and cover with the remaining cake mixture. Scatter over the remaining streusel mixture and press down lightly.

6. Bake in the centre of the oven for about 45–60 minutes or until the top springs back when pressed lightly with a fingertip. Allow to cool in the tin for a few minutes, then turn out on to a wire rack and leave to cool completely.

♦ ♦

Peanut Cake

melted lard or oil for greasing tin
3 eggs
85g/3oz caster sugar
85g/3oz plain flour
½ teaspoon baking powder
85g/3oz butter, melted and cooled
110g/4oz peanuts, toasted, skinned and ground

To serve
3 tablespoons orange curd
  (see page 154)   } mixed together
55g/2oz cream cheese

To finish
icing sugar, sifted

1. Preheat the oven to 180°C/350°F/gas mark 4. Grease a 20cm/8in moule-à-manqué tin and line the base with a disc of greased greaseproof paper.

2. Whisk the eggs with the sugar until light and fluffy.

3. Sift the flour with the baking powder and mix with the ground peanuts. Fold into the egg and sugar mixture, using a large metal spoon. Pour the cool butter on to the mixture and fold in carefully. Pour into the prepared tin.

4. Bake in the centre of the oven for 30–35 minutes or until the top feels firm to the touch.

5. Remove from the oven and allow to cool in the tin for 10 minutes, then turn out on to a wire rack and leave to cool completely.

6. When the cake is cold, split in half horizontally and sandwich together with the orange curd and cream cheese mixed together. Dust the top with icing sugar.

NOTE: This cake will keep in the refrigerator for 2-3 days.

♦ ♦

Coconut Fruit Cake

This recipe was given to me by David Scott Bradbury, the manager of Leith's Restaurant. It is a rich and crumbly cake and will be enjoyed by coconut lovers.

melted lard or oil for greasing tin
225g/8oz butter
325g/12oz caster sugar
4 eggs, beaten
450g/1lb self-raising flour, sifted
150ml/5fl oz milk
225g/8oz white or pale sultanas
225g/8oz citron peel, chopped, or chopped
    mixed peel
225g/8oz candied lemon peel, chopped
450g/1lb tin of pineapple, drained and chopped
450g/1lb brazil nuts, chopped
225g/8oz glacé cherries
225g/8oz fine desiccated coconut

1. Preheat the oven to 150°C/300°F/gas mark 2. Grease and flour a 23cm/9in deep cake tin. Line the base with a disc of greased greaseproof paper. Wrap several layers of newspaper around the outside of the tin (see page 30).
2. Cream the butter and sugar together in a large mixing bowl until light and fluffy. Add the eggs gradually, beating well after each addition.
3. Fold in the flour, using a large metal spoon, and add the milk. Stir in all the remaining ingredients and mix well. Turn into the prepared tin.
4. Bake in the oven for about 4 hours or until a sharp knife or skewer inserted into the centre of the cake comes out clear. If the top is getting too dark, cover with a piece of kitchen foil or greaseproof paper.
5. Remove the cake from the oven and allow to cool completely in the tin before turning out.

6 CAKES WITH VEGETABLES

Vegetables, particularly root vegetables, are very good in cakes as they add extra sweetness and an interesting texture.

♦ ♦

Carrot Cake

melted lard or oil for greasing tin
285g/10oz plain flour
2 teaspoons bicarbonate of soda
a pinch of salt
2 teaspoons ground cinnamon
225g/8oz caster sugar
3 eggs
225g/8oz butter, melted and cooled
2 teaspoons vanilla essence
225g/8oz carrots, grated

1. Preheat the oven to 170°C/325°F/gas mark 3. Grease a 900g/2lb loaf tin and line the base with a piece of greased greaseproof paper.

2. Sift the flour, bicarbonate of soda, salt and cinnamon together into a large mixing bowl. Add the sugar.
3. Whisk the eggs lightly with the butter and vanilla essence.
4. Make a well in the dry ingredients, add the egg and butter mixture and mix in carefully. Beat well and stir in the carrots. Mix thoroughly. Turn into the prepared tin.
5. Bake in the top of the oven for 1½–2 hours or until the top springs back when pressed lightly with a fingertip.
6. Remove the cake from the oven and allow to cool in the tin for 5 minutes, then turn out on to a wire rack and leave to cool completely.

♦ ♦

Austrian Carrot Cake

This is adapted from a recipe in Barbara Maher's *Cakes*.

melted lard or oil for greasing tin
5 eggs
225g/8oz caster sugar plus 1 extra teaspoon
225g/8oz carrots, finely grated
225g/8oz ground almonds
2 tablespoons rum
grated zest of 1 lemon
55g/2oz potato flour
1 teaspoon baking powder
1 teaspoon ground cinnamon
a pinch of ground cloves

To finish
icing sugar, sifted

1. Preheat the oven to 180°C/350°F/gas mark 4. Grease a 22cm/9in moule-à-manqué tin and line with a disc of greased greaseproof paper. Dust lightly with flour and tap out excess.
2. Separate the eggs. Beat the yolks and sugar together in a large bowl until pale.
3. Whisk the egg whites until stiff. Whisk in the remaining teaspoon of sugar and fold into the yolk and sugar mixture, using a large metal spoon.
4. Carefully fold in the carrots, ground almonds, rum and lemon zest. Sift the flour, baking powder, cinnamon and cloves together into the mixture and combine carefully and thoroughly. Pour into the prepared tin.
5. Bake in the centre of the oven for about 50 minutes or until the top springs back when pressed lightly with a fingertip.
6. Remove the cake from the oven and allow to cool in the tin for 5 minutes, then turn out on to a wire rack and leave to cool completely. Dust lightly with icing sugar before serving.

◆ ◆

Boiled Carrot Cake

melted lard or oil for greasing tin
170g/6oz carrots, grated
110g/4oz raisins
55g/2oz dried apricots, chopped
150ml/5fl oz water
200g/7oz caster sugar
30g/1oz butter
225g/8oz self-raising flour
½ teaspoon ground cinnamon
½ teaspoon ground cloves
85g/3oz walnuts, chopped

1. Preheat the oven to 170°C/325°F/gas mark 3. Grease a 900g/2lb loaf tin and line the base with a piece of greased greaseproof paper.
2. Put the carrots, raisins, apricots, water, sugar and butter together into a saucepan. Place over a low heat until the sugar has dissolved completely, then bring to the boil, cover with a lid and simmer for 10 minutes. Remove from the heat and allow to cool for about 45 minutes.
3. Sift the flour with the spices and add to the cooled mixture with the chopped walnuts, to make a fairly sloppy batter. Pour into the prepared tin.

4. Bake in the centre of the oven for 1–1¼ hours or until a sharp knife or skewer inserted into the centre of the cake comes out clean.

5. Remove the cake from the oven and allow to cool for 10 minutes in the tin, then turn out on to a wire rack and leave to cool completely.

◆ ◆

Parsnip Bread

melted lard or butter for greasing tin
285g/10oz plain flour
2 teaspoons bicarbonate of soda
a pinch of salt
1 teaspoon ground mixed spice
1 teaspoon ground ginger
225g/8oz caster sugar
3 eggs
225g/8oz butter, melted and cooled
2 teaspoons vanilla essence
225g/8oz parsnips, grated

1. Preheat the oven to 170°C/325°F/gas mark 3. Grease a 900g/2lb loaf tin and line the base with a piece of greased greaseproof paper.

2. Sift the flour, bicarbonate of soda, salt, mixed spice and ginger together into a large mixing bowl. Add the sugar.

3. Whisk the eggs lightly with the butter and vanilla essence.

4. Make a well in the dry ingredients, add the egg and butter mixture and mix in carefully. Beat well, then stir in the grated parsnips. Mix thoroughly. Turn into the prepared tin.

5. Bake in the top of the oven for 1½–2 hours or until the top springs back when pressed lightly with a fingertip.

6. Remove the loaf from the oven and allow to cool in the tin for 5 minutes, then turn out on to a wire rack and leave to cool completely.

◆ ◆

Parsnip and Pecan Cake

This is an all-in-one recipe and therefore quick and easy to make. It does not rise very much. If a deep cake is required, double the quantities and bake in 2 tins. Sandwich the cakes together with the icing and dust with icing sugar before serving.

For the cake
melted lard or oil for greasing tin
140g/5oz plain flour
2 teaspoons baking powder
140g/5oz parsnips, grated
55g/2oz pecan nuts, chopped
1 teaspoon freshly grated root ginger
1 egg, lightly beaten
a pinch of salt
150ml/5fl oz sunflower oil
140g/5oz caster sugar

For the icing
85g/3oz unsalted butter, softened
110g/4oz cream cheese
55g/2oz icing sugar
2 tablespoons orange juice
peeled zest of 1 orange, cut into thin strips
2 tablespoons sugar
100ml/4fl oz water

1. Preheat the oven to 180°C/350°F/gas mark 4. Grease a 20cm/8in moule-à-manqué or sandwich tin. Line the base with a disc of greased greaseproof paper.
2. Put all the cake ingredients into a large mixing bowl and mix together thoroughly. Turn into the prepared tin.
3. Bake in the centre of the oven for about 30 minutes or until a sharp knife or skewer inserted into the centre of the cake comes out clean.
4. Remove the cake from the oven and leave to cool completely in the tin.
5. Meanwhile, make the icing: put the butter into a bowl and beat, gradually add the cream cheese, beating all the time. Add the icing sugar and orange juice and continue beating until light and fluffy. Chill in the refrigerator.
6. Put the water and sugar into a small saucepan and heat slowly until all the sugar has dissolved. Add the orange zest, bring to the boil and boil for 5 minutes. Using a slotted spoon, remove the zest and leave on a plate to cool.
7. When the cake is cold, spread with the icing and decorate with the orange zest.

◆ ◆

Rich Chocolate Squash Cake

oil for greasing tin
225g/8oz raw gem squash or courgettes, grated
110g/4oz unsalted butter, softened
55ml/2fl oz sunflower oil
85g/3oz soft dark brown sugar, sifted
2 large eggs
55g/2oz cocoa powder
110g/4oz plain flour
1 teaspoon baking powder
1 teaspoon bicarbonate of soda
½ teaspoon ground cloves
1 teaspoon ground cinnamon
55ml/2fl oz water
110g/4oz plain chocolate buttons
55g/2oz pistachio nuts, shelled

To finish
icing sugar, sifted

1. Preheat the oven to 180°C/350°F/gas mark 4. Lightly oil a 900g/2lb loaf tin and line the base with a piece of oiled greaseproof paper.
2. Put the squash or courgettes into a clean J-cloth or tea towel and wring out all the excess moisture until completely dry. Put into a bowl and fork through to separate the strands.
3. Put the butter, oil and sugar into a mixing bowl and beat until light and fluffy.
4. Separate the eggs and beat the yolks into the creamed mixture.
5. Sift the cocoa powder, flour, baking powder, bicarbonate of soda and spices together on to the butter mixture and fold

in, using a large metal spoon. Stir in the water gently.

6. Add the chocolate buttons, squash or courgettes and pistachios and mix well.

7. Whisk the egg whites until stiff but not dry. Fold the whites quickly into the cake mixture, without knocking out too much air. Turn into the prepared tin and smooth the top with a spatula.

8. Bake in the centre of the preheated oven for about 40–45 minutes or until a sharp knife or skewer inserted into the centre of the cake comes out clean.

9. Remove the cake from the oven and allow to cool completely in the tin.

10. When the cake is cold, remove from the tin and serve dusted with icing sugar.

♦ ♦

Pumpkin Bread

melted lard or oil for greasing tins
325g/12oz caster sugar
400g/14oz plain flour
1 teaspoon bicarbonate of soda
¼ teaspoon salt
¼ teaspoon ground cloves
1 teaspoon freshly grated nutmeg
½ teaspoon ground cinnamon
110ml/4fl oz sunflower oil
2 eggs, beaten
225g/8oz canned pumpkin purée
150ml/5fl oz water
85g/3oz walnuts, chopped
110g/4oz dates, chopped

1. Preheat the oven to 180°C/350°F/gas

mark 4. Grease two 675g/1½lb loaf tins and line the base of each with a piece of greased greaseproof paper.

2. Sift the sugar, flour, bicarbonate of soda, salt and spices together into a large mixing bowl. Make a well in the centre.

3. Add the oil, eggs, pumpkin purée and water and mix very well, beating out any lumps. Stir in the walnuts and dates. Pour into the prepared tins.

4. Bake in the centre of the oven for about 1 hour or until the tops spring back when pressed lightly with a fingertip.

5. Remove the loaves from the oven and allow to cool in the tins for 10 minutes, then turn out on to a wire rack and leave to cool completely.

♦ ♦

Pumpkin and Banana Bread

melted lard or oil for greasing tins
450g/1lb pumpkin, steamed and cooled or
   400g/14oz canned pumpkin purée
2 ripe bananas
2 eggs
340g/12oz caster sugar
290ml/½ pint sunflower oil
550g/1¼lb plain flour
1 tablespoon baking powder
½ teaspoon ground ginger
2 teaspoons ground cinnamon
1 teaspoon salt
225g/8oz walnuts, chopped

For the icing
225g/8oz cream cheese
30g/1oz caster sugar

To decorate
chopped walnuts
grated lemon zest

1. Preheat the oven to 180°C/350°F/gas mark 4. Grease two 900g/2lb loaf tins and line the base of each with a piece of greased greaseproof paper.
2. Mash the pumpkin and banana together in a large mixing bowl. Beat in the eggs, sugar and oil.
3. Sift together the flour, baking powder, spices and salt. Beat into the pumpkin mixture until thoroughly mixed. Stir in the walnuts. Divide the mixture between the prepared tins.
4. Bake in the centre of the oven for about 1 hour or until a sharp knife or skewer inserted into the centre of the loaves comes out clean.
5. Meanwhile, make the icing: mix the cream cheese with the sugar. It may be necessary to add more sugar as some cream cheeses are very salty. The mixture should taste slightly sweet, not savoury.
6. When the loaves are cold, spread the cream cheese icing over the top and decorate with walnuts and lemon zest.

◆ ◆ ◆ ◆ ◆ ◆ ◆ ◆ ◆ ◆ ◆ ◆ ◆ ◆ ◆ ◆ ◆ ◆ ◆ ◆

Courgette Bread

melted lard or oil for greasing tin
170g/6oz plain flour
2 teaspoons baking powder
1 teaspoon bicarbonate of soda
1 teaspoon salt
1 teaspoon ground cinnamon
1 teaspoon ground cloves
a pinch of freshly grated nutmeg
2 eggs
170g/6oz sugar

85ml/3fl oz sunflower oil
1 teaspoon vanilla essence
225g/8oz courgettes, grated
85g/3oz walnuts, chopped

1. Preheat the oven to 170°C/325°F/gas mark 3. Grease a 900g/2lb loaf tin and line the base with a piece of greased greaseproof paper.
2. Sift the flour, baking powder, bicarbonate of soda, salt, and spices together into a large mixing bowl.

3. Beat the eggs lightly and add the sugar, oil and vanilla essence. Add the courgettes and walnuts.

4. Make a well in the centre of the flour and pour in the egg mixture. Mix in well. Pour into the prepared tin.

5. Bake in the centre of the oven for about 1½ hours or until a sharp knife or skewer inserted into the centre of the loaf comes out clean.

6. Remove the loaf from the oven and allow to cool in the tin for 10 minutes, then turn out on to a wire rack and leave to cool completely.

NOTE: The bread must be left undisturbed in the oven for 1¼ hours. If the oven door is opened before the bread has set, it will sink in the centre.

◆ ◆

Ginger and Lemon Cake

This cake is made with grated raw potato. It is lovely and moist, with a slightly chewy crust.

melted lard or oil for greasing tin
170g/6oz butter
170g/6oz soft dark brown sugar
3 eggs, beaten
170g/6oz self-raising flour
2 teaspoons ground ginger
2 teaspoons ground cinnamon
110g/4oz grated potato

For the icing
170g/6oz icing sugar, sifted
2 tablespoons lemon juice
1 teaspoon finely grated lemon zest

1. Preheat the oven to 180°C/350°F/gas mark 4. Grease a 450g/1lb loaf tin and line the base with a piece of greased greaseproof paper.

2. Cream the butter and sugar together in a mixing bowl until light and fluffy. Add the eggs gradually, beating well after each addition. Add a little of the flour if necessary to prevent the mixture from curdling.

3. Sift the flour and spices together on to the mixture and fold in, using a large metal spoon. Fold in the grated potato. Turn into the prepared tin.

4. Bake in the centre of the oven for 50–60 minutes or until the top springs back when pressed lightly with a fingertip.

5. When the cake is cold, make the icing: mix the icing sugar with the lemon juice and zest. Spread on top of the cake.

NOTE: The cake will keep well for 4–5 days in a tin or it can be frozen.

7   PICNIC CAKES

Although many other cakes in the book are good to take on picnics, the ones in this chapter are particularly transportable. Being substantial, they are perfect for keen appetites in the open air, and as they all have very good keeping qualities, they can be made well in advance.

♦ ♦

Coffee and Raisin Cake

melted lard or oil for greasing tin
140g/5oz soft light brown sugar
225g/8oz golden syrup
225g/8oz butter
2 teaspoons instant coffee
200ml/7fl oz boiling water
340g/12oz plain flour
½ teaspoon freshly grated nutmeg
½ teaspoon ground cloves
½ teaspoon ground cinnamon
1 teaspoon bicarbonate of soda
225g/8oz raisins
2 eggs, beaten

1. Preheat the oven to 160°C/325°F/gas mark 3. Grease a 20cm/8in deep cake tin and line with a disc of greased greaseproof paper.
2. Put the sugar, syrup and butter into a medium saucepan and melt over a low heat. Do not allow to boil.
3. Mix the coffee with the boiling water and allow to cool.
4. Sift the flour, nutmeg, cloves, cinnamon and bicarbonate of soda together into a large mixing bowl. Add the raisins and make a well in the centre.
5. Pour in the melted mixture, coffee and eggs and mix thoroughly but carefully. Pour into the prepared tin.
6. Bake in the centre of the oven for about 1½ hours or until a sharp knife or skewer inserted into the centre of the cake comes out clean.
7. Remove from the oven and allow to cool in the tin for 10 minutes, then turn on to a wire rack and leave to cool completely.

NOTE: This cake keeps very well and will be at its best 1–2 weeks after it is baked if stored in an airtight tin.

◆ ◆

Fig and Oat Loaf

This cake is delicious when cut into slices
and spread with butter.

melted lard or oil for greasing tin
225g/8oz butter
225g/8oz soft light brown sugar
225g/8oz golden syrup
340g/12oz plain flour
1 teaspoon ground ginger
1 teaspoon ground cinnamon
1 teaspoon ground cardamom
1 teaspoon ground coriander
1 teaspoon freshly grated nutmeg
85g/3oz no-need-to-soak dried figs, chopped
55g/2oz porridge oats
2 eggs, beaten
150ml/5fl oz milk
2 teaspoons bicarbonate of soda

1. Preheat the oven to 150°C/300°F/gas
mark 2. Grease a 900g/2lb loaf tin and line
the base with a piece of greased greaseproof
paper.
2. Melt the butter, sugar and syrup together
in a saucepan.
3. Sift the flour and spices together into a
bowl. Add the figs and oats. Make a well in
the centre and add the melted mixture and
the eggs. Warm the milk to blood heat, add
the bicarbonate of soda, stir well and pour
into the well, stirring all the time. Using a
wooden spoon, gradually draw in the dry
ingredients from the sides, and beat until
smooth.
4. Bake in the centre of the oven for about
1½ hours or until a sharp knife or skewer
inserted into the centre comes out clean.
5. Remove from the oven and allow to cool
in the tin for 10 minutes, then turn out on to
a wire rack and leave to cool completely.

◆ ◆

Honey Cake

melted lard or oil for greasing tin
140g/5oz butter
110g/4oz soft light brown sugar
170g/6oz clear honey
2 eggs, beaten
225g/8oz self-raising flour, sifted
15g/½oz flaked almonds

1. Preheat the oven to 180°C/350°F/gas
mark 4. Grease a 900g/2lb loaf tin and line
the base with a piece of greased greaseproof
paper.

2. Put the butter, sugar and honey into a
medium saucepan and melt over a low heat.
Remove from the heat and allow to cool.
Beat in the eggs. Fold in the flour carefully,
using a large metal spoon.
3. Pour into the prepared tin and spread out
evenly. Sprinkle the surface with the
almonds.
4. Bake in the centre of the oven for 45
minutes or until the top springs back when
pressed lightly with a fingertip.
5. Remove from the oven and allow to cool
in the tin for 10 minutes, then turn out on to
a wire rack and leave to cool completely.

♦ ♦

Black Sticky Gingerbread

This gingerbread keeps very well: in fact it improves with keeping.

melted lard or oil for greasing tin
225g/8oz butter
225g/8oz soft light brown sugar
225g/8oz black treacle
340g/12oz plain flour
2 teaspoons ground ginger
1 tablespoon ground cinnamon
2 eggs, beaten
290ml/½ pint milk
2 teaspoons bicarbonate of soda

1. Preheat the oven to 150°C/300°F/gas mark 2. Grease a 30 × 20cm/12 × 8in roasting tin and line the base with a piece of greased greaseproof paper.
2. Melt the butter, sugar and treacle together in a saucepan over a low heat. Do not allow to boil.
3. Sift the flour with the spices into a mixing bowl and make a well in the centre. Pour in the melted mixture with the eggs. Warm the milk to blood heat, add the bicarbonate of soda and stir into the mixture. Stir well and pour the mixture into the prepared tin.
4. Bake in the centre of the oven for about 1½ hours or until a sharp knife or skewer inserted into the centre comes out clean. Cover the top with a piece of greaseproof paper after 1 hour.
5. Remove from the oven and allow to cool for 10 minutes, then turn on to a wire rack and leave to cool completely.
6. When gingerbread is cold, cut it into fingers and serve spread with butter.

♦ ♦

Ginger Cake

This gingerbread is dark and sticky and keeps very well. It improves if it is kept for a week before serving. Do not open the oven door during baking or the cake will sink. It may sink a little after baking but will be delicious none the less.

melted lard or oil for greasing tin
110g/4oz butter
110g/4oz soft dark brown sugar
225g/8oz black treacle
225g/8oz plain flour
1 teaspoon ground ginger
2 eggs, beaten
55g/2oz sultanas
55g/2oz preserved ginger, chopped
2 tablespoons milk
½ teaspoon bicarbonate of soda

1. Preheat the oven to 160°C/325°F/gas mark 3. Grease an 18cm/7in cake tin and line the base with a disc of greased

greaseproof paper.

2. Melt the butter, sugar and treacle in a saucepan over a low heat. Do not let the mixture boil. Remove from the heat and allow to cool slightly.

3. Sift the flour with the ginger into a mixing bowl and make a well in the centre. Pour in the melted mixture and the eggs. Using a wooden spoon, gradually draw in the flour and mix carefully and well to a smooth batter. Add the sultanas and preserved ginger. Warm the milk to blood heat, stir in the bicarbonate of soda and mix in quickly. Pour into the prepared tin.

4. Bake in the centre of the oven for 1½ hours or until the top springs back when pressed lightly with a fingertip.

5. Remove from the oven and cool in the tin for 15 minutes, then turn out on to a wire rack and leave to cool completely.

NOTE: If the cake is to be kept for a few days before serving, wrap in kitchen foil or store in an airtight cake tin.

8   SLICES AND BISCUITS

As these are easy to make and freeze and store well, they are ideal if you are baking for a picnic, sale of work, fête or cricket tea.

◆ ◆

Fruit Slices

MAKES 18

melted lard or oil for greasing tin
85g/3oz butter
55g/2oz caster sugar
2 eggs
225g/8oz plain flour
1 teaspoon baking powder
½ teaspoon vanilla essence
½ teaspoon ground mixed spice
a pinch of ground cloves
110g/4oz dried dates, chopped
55g/2oz pitted prunes, chopped
55g/2oz dried apricots, chopped
55g/2oz chopped mixed peel
110g/4oz hazelnuts, toasted, skinned and
   chopped
55g/2oz plain chocolate, chopped
85g/3oz raisins
grated zest and juice of 1 orange
100ml/3½fl oz milk

For the icing
110g/4oz plain chocolate, chopped
20g/¾oz butter

1. Preheat the oven to 180°C/350°F/gas mark 4. Grease a small roasting tin measuring about 28 × 22.5cm/11 × 9in and line the base with a piece of greased greaseproof paper.
2. Cream the butter and sugar together in a mixing bowl until light and creamy. Add the eggs gradually, beating well after each addition. Sift together the flour and baking powder and fold into the mixture with the vanilla essence, mixed spice and cloves. Stir in the chopped fruit, nuts, chocolate, raisins, orange zest and juice and the milk. Turn into the prepared tin and spread out evenly.
3. Bake in the oven for 45 minutes. Remove from the oven and allow to cool in the tin.
4. When the cake is cold, make the icing: melt the chocolate and butter in a heatproof bowl over (not in) a saucepan of gently simmering water. Allow to cool slightly, then spread over the top of the cake. Allow to set, then cut into 18 even pieces.

◆ ◆

Walnut and Coconut Slices

MAKES 12

For the base
melted lard or oil for greasing tin
85g/3oz self-raising flour
55g/2oz caster sugar
55g/2oz butter, melted and cooled
45g/1½oz desiccated coconut

For the topping
2 eggs
½ teaspoon vanilla essence
85g/3oz desiccated coconut
85g/3oz walnuts, chopped
225g/8oz soft light brown sugar
½ teaspoon baking powder

1. Preheat the oven to 180°C/350°F/gas mark 4. Grease a shallow 25 × 20cm/ 10 × 8in tin.
2. Make the base: mix the flour, sugar, melted butter and coconut together in a mixing bowl. This will produce a crumbly mixture, so use your hands to bring it together and then press it into the base of the prepared tin, using the back of a spoon to make sure it is level and pressed into the corners. Chill in the refrigerator for 10 minutes.
3. Bake in the centre of the oven for about 10 minutes or until beginning to brown. Remove from the oven and allow to cool in the tin for 10–15 minutes.
4. Meanwhile, make the topping: beat the eggs with the vanilla essence until they are well broken up. Add all the remaining ingredients and mix well.
5. Spread the mixture over the base and return to the oven. Bake for 15 minutes, then turn the oven temperature down to 170°C/325°F/gas mark 3 and bake for 20 further minutes or until the topping is brown and still feels slightly soft when pressed lightly with a fingertip.
6. Remove from the oven and allow to cool in the tin for 15 minutes. Mark the cake into 12 even pieces. Transfer to a wire rack and leave to cool completely. When cold cut into the marked pieces.

◆ ◆

Nut Squares

These squares have the sticky consistency of pecan pie. They can be made using pecan nuts or hazelnuts or a combination of the two. They will keep for about 5 days in a tin or will freeze very well.

MAKES 20

For the biscuit base
melted lard or oil for greasing tin
85g/3oz butter
85g/3oz sugar
1 egg, beaten
a few drops of vanilla essence
1 teaspoon grated lemon zest
170g/6oz plain flour

For the nut topping
170g/6oz nuts, such as pecan nuts, hazelnuts or
   a combination of both, chopped
375g/12oz soft light brown sugar
55g/2oz plain chocolate, grated
3 eggs, beaten
2 tablespoons plain flour

1. Preheat the oven to 180°C/350°F/gas mark 4. Grease a 30 × 22cm/12 × 9in roasting tin.
2 Make the biscuit base: cream the butter in a mixing bowl and add the sugar. Beat together until pale and fluffy. Add the egg, vanilla essence and lemon zest and beat well. Stir in the flour.
3. Spread the mixture evenly in the prepared tin. Chill in the refrigerator for 10 minutes.
4. Bake the biscuit base in the centre of the oven for 10 minutes.
5. Meanwhile, make the topping: mix together the nuts, sugar, chocolate and eggs. Beat well and stir in the flour.
6. Remove the biscuit base from the oven and pour over the nut topping. Turn up the oven temperature to 190°C/375°F/gas mark 5 and bake for 30 minutes.
7. Remove from the oven and allow to cool completely in the tin. Cut into even squares or fingers.

◆ ◆

Orange Oatmeal Squares

MAKES 20

For the base:
melted lard or oil for greasing tin
290ml/½ pint orange juice
110g/4oz rolled oats
110g/4oz butter
170g/6oz soft dark brown sugar

2 eggs, beaten
225g/8oz self-raising flour
½ teaspoon ground cinnamon
55g/2oz walnuts, chopped

For the topping
110g/4oz soft dark brown sugar
55g/2oz butter
150ml/5fl oz orange juice
55g/2oz walnuts, chopped
55g/2oz flaked almonds

1. Preheat the oven to 180°C/350°F/gas mark 4. Grease a 30 × 22cm/12 × 9in shallow tin and line the base with a piece of greased greaseproof paper.

2. Make the base: put the orange juice into a saucepan and bring to the boil. Reduce the heat and allow to simmer for 2 minutes. Pour over the oats in a bowl and stir well to mix. Set aside to cool.

3. Cream the butter in a mixing bowl. Add the sugar and beat well together until pale and fluffy. Add the eggs gradually, beating well after each addition.

4. Sift the flour with the cinnamon. Fold half the flour mixture into the creamed mixture. Blend in the cool, soaked oatmeal and orange juice. Mix carefully to ensure there are no lumps. Fold in the remaining flour and stir in the walnuts. Pour into the prepared tin and spread out evenly.

5. Bake in the centre of the oven for 30 minutes or until the top springs back when pressed lightly with a fingertip. Remove from the oven and allow to cool in the tin.

6. Meanwhile, make the topping: put the sugar, butter and orange juice into a saucepan. Bring to the boil and dissolve the sugar, then reduce the heat and allow to simmer for 8 minutes. Add the walnuts and almonds and simmer for 1 further minute, taking care that the mixture does not burn. Remove from the heat and allow to cool for 10 minutes.

7. Preheat the grill to its highest setting.

8. Spread the topping over the cooled base and place under the grill for about 1 minute or until bubbling on top. Watch carefully in case it shows signs of burning. Allow to cool in the tin, then cut into squares.

NOTE: The topping becomes very hot when it is grilled. Do not be tempted to pick a piece off the top at this stage.

♦ ♦

Millionaire's Shortbread

MAKES 16

For the shortbread
melted lard or oil for greasing tin
200g/7oz butter
110g/4oz caster sugar
285g/10oz plain flour

For the filling
110g/4oz butter
110g/4oz caster sugar

2 tablespoons golden syrup
1 × 400g/14oz can condensed milk

For the topping
110g/4oz plain chocolate, chopped

1. Preheat the oven to 180°C/350°F/gas mark 4. Grease a 30 × 22cm/12 × 9in Swiss roll tin.

2. Make the shortbread: cream the butter in a mixing bowl, add the sugar and beat until light and fluffy. Add the flour and bring together to form a dough.

3. Press the dough evenly into the prepared tin, using the back of a spoon.

4. Bake in the centre of the oven for 20 minutes or until golden-brown. Remove from the oven and allow to cool completely in the tin.

5. Make the filling: put all the ingredients into a saucepan and heat gently to melt the butter and dissolve the sugar, stirring occasionally. Increase the heat and boil rapidly for 5 minutes, stirring constantly. Remove from the heat and allow to cool for

1 minute. Pour over the cooled shortbread. Allow to cool and set.

6. Make the topping: melt the chocolate in a small heatproof bowl over (not in) a saucepan of gently simmering water. Spread the melted chocolate carefully over the cold set caramel. Mark into fingers and leave to set before removing from the tin. Cut into fingers only once they are cold.

◆ ◆

Coffee Streusel Bars

MAKES 16

For the base
melted lard or oil for greasing tin
110g//4oz butter
55g/2oz caster sugar
170g/6oz plain flour

For the filling
1 × 400g/14oz can sweetened condensed milk
30g/1oz butter
2 tablespoons golden syrup
3 teaspoons instant coffee
55g/2oz walnuts, chopped

For the topping
170g/6oz plain flour
110g/4oz butter
2 teaspoons ground cinnamon
55g/2oz soft, light brown sugar

1. Preheat the oven to 180°C/350°F/gas mark 4. Grease a 30 × 22cm/12 × 9in shallow tin.

2. Make the base: cream the butter and sugar together in a mixing bowl until pale and fluffy. Stir in the flour and bring together to form a dough.

3. Press the dough evenly into the prepared tin, using the back of a spoon.

4. Bake in the centre of the oven for 10 minutes.

5. Meanwhile, make the filling: put the condensed milk, butter, syrup and coffee into a saucepan and stir together over a medium heat. Bring to the boil, then reduce the heat and simmer for about 3 minutes or until thick. Stir in the walnuts. Cool.

6. Remove the base from the oven and spread evenly with the filling mixture.

7. Make the topping: sift the flour into a bowl. Cut the butter into the flour and rub in carefully with the fingertips, ensuring the butter does not get too soft. Stir in the cinnamon and sugar.

8. Sprinkle the topping over the surface of the filling. Return to the oven and bake for 15 further minutes or until firm to the touch.

9. Remove from the oven and allow to cool completely in the tin before cutting into slices.

◆ ◆

Panforte

This is a rich, chewy Italian delicacy. It is a cross between a cake and a biscuit and is traditionally served with strong black coffee, often at Christmas. Store in an airtight container for up to 2 weeks.

rice paper
170g/6oz granulated sugar
170g/6oz clear honey
170g/6oz blanched almonds
110g/4oz walnuts, chopped
110g/4oz hazelnuts, chopped
110g/4oz dried figs, chopped
110g/4oz chopped mixed peel
55g/2oz glacé cherries, chopped
55g/2oz glacé pineapple, chopped
85g/3oz plain flour
30g/1oz cocoa
1 teaspoon ground cinnamon
¼ teaspoon freshly grated nutmeg

To finish
1 tablespoon icing sugar
½ teaspoon ground cinnamon

1. Preheat the oven to 180°C/350°F/gas mark 4. Line the base and sides of a 23cm/9in sandwich tin with rice paper, cutting it to fit exactly.
2. Heat the sugar and honey together gently, stirring all the time until the sugar dissolves. Bring to the boil, then reduce the heat and simmer for 2 minutes. Remove from the heat and allow to cool slightly.
3. Mix together the chopped nuts and fruit. Sift together the flour, cocoa and spices and mix with the nuts and fruit. Add the cooled syrup and stir well to combine thoroughly.
4. Spoon the mixture into the prepared tin, cover with another piece of rice paper and flatten the top.
5. Bake in the centre of the oven for 45–60 minutes or until fairly firm to the touch but not solid.
6. Remove from the oven and allow to cool in the tin for 20 minutes, then carefully ease out of the tin and transfer to a wire rack. Leave to cool completely.
7. Sift the icing sugar and cinnamon together over the top before serving.

◆ ◆

Peanut Brownies

These are a cross between a cake and a biscuit.

MAKES ABOUT 20
melted lard or oil for greasing baking sheet
110g/4oz butter
170g/6oz caster sugar
2 tablespoons cocoa powder
1 egg
170g/6oz self-raising flour
110g/4oz peanuts, toasted, skinned and chopped

1. Preheat the oven to 180°C/350°F/gas mark 4. Grease a baking sheet.
2. Melt the butter in a saucepan, add the sugar and cocoa and mix well. Allow to cool,

then beat in the egg. Fold in the flour and peanuts.

3. Using wet hands, shape the mixture into balls the size of a ping-pong ball and place on the baking sheet, allowing 2.5cm/1in between them for spreading.

4. Bake in the centre of the oven for about 15 minutes or until they spring back when pressed with a fingertip. Transfer to a wire rack and leave to cool completely. Store in an airtight container.

◆ ◆

Muesli Biscuits

MAKES ABOUT 40
melted lard or oil for greasing baking sheets
225g/8oz rolled oats
55g/2oz raisins
55g/2oz hazelnuts, toasted and chopped
55g/2oz almonds, toasted and chopped
110g/4oz dried apricots, chopped
110g/4oz self-raising flour
110g/4oz soft light brown sugar
55g/2oz sesame seeds
1 tablespoon clear honey
2 eggs, beaten
170g/6oz butter, melted and cooled

1. Preheat the oven to 180°C/350°F/gas mark 4. Grease 3 baking sheets.
2. Combine all the dry ingredients in a large bowl.
3. Mix together the honey, eggs and butter and add to the dry ingredients. Mix very well.
4. Put large teaspoons of the mixture on to a baking sheet, flattening them slightly and allowing 5cm/2in between them for spreading.
5. Bake in the oven for 10–15 minutes or until firm to the touch. Transfer to a wire rack and leave to cool completely. Store in an airtight container.

◆ ◆

Almond and Gin Biscuits

These biscuits have a wonderfully crisp texture and a delicious taste, with a very slight hint of juniper. They keep well in an airtight container – that is, if you can resist eating them all at once!

MAKES 14
melted lard or oil for greasing baking sheets
110g/4oz butter

85g/3oz caster sugar
2 tablespoons gin
140g/5oz plain flour, sifted
85g/3oz flaked almonds, chopped

1. Preheat the oven to 180°C/350°F/gas mark 4. Grease 2 baking sheets.
2. Cream the butter and sugar together in a mixing bowl until light and fluffy. Beat in the gin.
3. Mix together the sifted flour and almonds and stir into the butter mixture. Bring the dough together, first with a wooden spoon

and then with the fingers of one hand.

4. Shape into 14 balls approximately the size of a ping-pong ball.

5. Place on the baking sheets, allowing 5cm/2in between them for spreading. Press your thumb into the centre of each, to make a dimple.

6. Bake in the top of the oven for 15–20 minutes or until golden-brown. Transfer to a wire rack and leave to cool completely.

◆ ◆

Macaroons

MAKES 20

rice paper or silicone baking powder
110g/4oz ground almonds
170g/6oz caster sugar
1 teaspoon plain flour
2 egg whites
2 drops of vanilla essence

To decorate
split blanched almonds

1. Preheat the oven to 180°C/350°F/gas mark 4. Line a baking sheet with rice paper or silicone paper.

2. Mix together the almonds, sugar and flour.

3. Add the egg whites and vanilla. Beat very well.

4. Place teaspoonsful of the mixture on the baking sheet, allowing 5cm/2in between them for spreading. Place a split almond on each macaroon.

5. Bake in the oven for 20 minutes or until the macaroons are firm to the touch and the almonds are golden-brown. Transfer to a wire rack and leave to cool completely. Trim the excess paper from around the macaroons.

◆ ◆

Flapjacks

MAKES 18

melted lard or oil for greasing tin
170g/6oz butter
110g/4oz demerara sugar
55g/2oz golden syrup
225g/8oz rolled oats

1. Preheat the oven to 190°C/375°F/gas mark 5. Grease a 30 × 22cm/12 × 9in shallow tin.

2. Melt the butter in a saucepan. Add the sugar and syrup and heat through.

3. Remove the pan from the heat and stir in the oats. Spread the mixture evenly in the prepared tin.

4. Bake in the centre of the oven for about 30 minutes or until golden-brown.

5. Remove from the oven and mark immediately into bars. Allow to cool completely in the tin.

9   YEAST CAKES

The recipes in this section use fresh yeast. If using dried yeast use half the amount. Easy-blend yeast can be sprinkled directly on to the flour. Follow the directions on the packet.

When heating the liquid to mix with yeast, never allow it to get hotter than blood temperature (i.e. when you dip your finger into the liquid it feels only just warm). If too hot it will kill the yeast and the dough will not rise. It is better to err on the side of caution and have the liquid too cold.

◆ ◆

Selkirk Bannock

This is a round, flat, yeasted fruit loaf.

30g/1oz fresh yeast
225g/8oz sugar
110g/4oz butter
110g/4oz lard
570ml/1 pint lukewarm milk
900g/2lb plain flour
a pinch of salt
170g/6oz sultanas
170g/6oz raisins
110g/4oz chopped mixed peel

1. Cream the yeast with 1 teaspoon of the sugar.
2. Melt the butter and lard until liquid but not hot. Add to the milk with the yeast mixture.
3. Sift the flour with the salt into a large mixing bowl. Make a well in the centre to expose the bottom of the bowl. Pour the yeast mixture slowly into the well, mixing with a round-bladed knife and gradually drawing in the surrounding flour until you have a smooth, softish batter.
4. Cover the bowl with a piece of greased clingfilm or a clean damp cloth and leave in a warm place to rise until doubled in bulk. This should take about 1 hour, depending on the warmth of the room.
5. Preheat the oven to 200°C/400°F/gas mark 6.
6. Tip the risen dough on to a floured work surface and work in the dried fruits, peel and the remaining sugar, kneading carefully until the fruits are evenly distributed. Divide the dough in half and shape into large rounds. Place on a floured baking sheet.
7. Cover the dough once again with the clingfilm or cloth, return to the warm place and leave until 1½ times its original bulk. This will take about 15 minutes.

8. Bake in the oven for 35–40 minutes or until the loaves sound hollow when tapped on the underside. If the bannocks show signs of becoming too brown, turn the oven temperature down to 170°C/325°F/gas mark 3.

9. Transfer the bannocks to a wire rack and leave to cool.

◆ ◆

Barm Brack

Barm means yeast and brack means speckled. Barm Brack is a sweet Irish yeast bread traditionally served at Hallowe'en. The speckles are the caraway seeds.

melted lard or oil for greasing baking sheet
675g/1½lb plain flour
½ teaspoon salt
15g/½oz fresh yeast
½ teaspoon caster sugar
290ml/½ pint lukewarm water
2 eggs, lightly beaten
55g/2oz butter, melted and cooled
85g/3oz caster sugar
30g/1oz caraway seeds

1. Preheat the oven to 200°C/400°F/gas mark 6. Grease a baking sheet.

2. Sift the flour with the salt into a large mixing bowl. Make a well in the centre.

3. Cream the yeast with the sugar and some of the water.

4. Add the yeast mixture, eggs and remaining water to the well in the flour. Mix to a soft dough, first with a round-bladed knife and then with the fingers of one hand. Knead for about 5 minutes or until the dough is smooth and elastic. Place in a large clean bowl, cover with greased clingfilm or a clean damp cloth and leave in a warm place to rise until doubled in bulk. This will take about 1 hour, depending on the warmth of the room.

5. Knock back the risen dough and knead in the butter, sugar and caraway seeds. Shape into a round loaf and place on the prepared baking sheet. Cover with greased clingfilm or a clean cloth, return to the warm place and leave for about 20 minutes or until 1½ times its original bulk.

6. Dust with a little flour, then bake in the centre of the oven. Bake for 30 minutes or until the loaf sounds hollow when tapped on the underside. Transfer to a wire rack to cool.

◆ ◆

Lardy Cake

450g/1lb flour
1 teaspoon salt
20g/³⁄₄oz fresh yeast
290ml/½ pint lukewarm water
melted lard for greasing tin
110g/4oz lard, cut into small pieces
110g/4oz sultanas
110g/4oz caster sugar
1 teaspoon ground mixed spice

To finish
2 tablespoons sugar

1. Sift the flour with the salt into a large mixing bowl. Cream the yeast with the water. Make a well in the centre of the flour and add the yeast mixture. Mix to a soft but not sticky dough, first with a round-bladed knife and then with the fingers of one hand. Knead quickly until the dough is smooth. Place in a large clean bowl, cover with greased clingfilm or a clean damp cloth, and leave in a warm place to rise until doubled in bulk. This will take about 1 hour, depending on the warmth of the room.
2. Preheat the oven to 200°C/400°F/gas mark 6. Grease a 25 × 20cm/10 × 8in roasting tin.
3. Place the risen dough on a floured work surface and roll out to a 45 × 15cm/18 × 6in rectangle.
4. Dot one-third of the lard over the top two-thirds of the dough. Toss the sultanas in the sugar and spice and sprinkle one-third of the mixture over the larded dough. Fold the dough into 3, bringing the bottom uncovered third up over the centre section first, and then the top third down over it.
5. Allow the dough to rest for 10 minutes.
6. Roll out again and cover with the second third of the lard, fruit, spice and sugar as in step 4. Fold into 3 as before.
7. Allow the dough to rest for 10 minutes.
8. Roll out again and cover with the remaining third of the lard, fruit, spice and sugar as in step 4. Fold into 3 as before.
9. Roll the dough out to fit the prepared tin. Place in the tin, cover and leave at room temperature to rise until 1½ times its original bulk.
10. Brush with a little oil and sprinkle with the 2 tablespoons sugar. Using a large knife, make a criss-cross pattern on the top.
11. Bake in the centre of the oven for 20 minutes, then turn the oven temperature down to 180°C/350°F/gas mark 4 and bake for about 1–1¼ hours or until the cake sounds hollow when tapped on the underside. Transfer to a wire rack to cool.

♦ ♦

Saffron Cake

Saffron cake is particularly popular in Cornwall. This is because the Phoenicians traded saffron for Cornish tin. Nowadays saffron is so expensive that saffron cakes sold in bakeries usually contain only a very little saffron and are coloured with yellow food dye. Only cakes labelled 'genuine saffron cake' contain the real thing.

30 saffron strands
150ml/5fl oz boiling water
15g/½oz fresh yeast
110g/4oz caster sugar
85ml/3fl oz lukewarm milk
450g/1lb plain flour
½ teaspoon salt
¼ teaspoon freshly grated nutmeg
¼ teaspoon ground cinnamon
85g/3oz butter
85g/3oz lard
melted lard for greasing tin
110g/4oz sultanas
110g/4oz currants
30g/1oz mixed peel

To glaze
beaten egg

1. Soak the strands of saffron in the boiling water for about 2 hours.
2. Cream the yeast with 1 teaspoon of the sugar and add the milk.
3. Sift the flour, salt and spices together into a large mixing bowl. Cut the butter and lard into pieces and rub in with the fingertips.
4. Make a well in the centre and add the yeast mixture, saffron and saffron-flavoured water. Mix to a soft dough, first with a round-bladed knife and then with the fingers of one hand. Knead well until the dough is smooth and elastic. Place in a large clean bowl, cover with greased clingfilm or a clean damp cloth, and leave in a warm place to rise until doubled in bulk.
5. Preheat the oven to 190°C/375°F/gas mark 5 and grease a 900g/2lb loaf tin.
6. Take the risen dough out of the bowl, scatter over the remaining sugar and the dried fruit and peel. Knock back the dough and knead in the fruit, distributing evenly throughout the dough.
7. Shape into a loaf and put into the prepared tin. Cover, return to the warm place and leave until 1½ times its original bulk. This will take about 15 minutes, depending on the warmth of the room.
8. Glaze the top of the loaf with beaten egg and bake in the oven for 20 minutes, then turn the oven temperature down to 180°C/350°F/gas mark 4 and bake for 25 further minutes or until the cake sounds hollow when tapped on the underside.
9. Turn out on to a wire rack and leave to cool completely.

◆ ◆ ◆ ◆ ◆ ◆ ◆ ◆ ◆ ◆ ◆ ◆ ◆ ◆ ◆ ◆ ◆ ◆ ◆ ◆

Gugelhopf

340g/12oz plain flour
1 teaspoon salt
25g/scant 1oz fresh yeast
225ml/7½fl oz lukewarm milk
30g/1oz caster sugar plus extra for the tin
2 small eggs, beaten
110g/4oz butter, softened
110g/4oz mixed raisins and currants
30g/1oz flaked almonds
butter for greasing the tin

1. Sift the flour with the salt into a warmed mixing bowl. Make a well in the centre.
2. Dissolve the yeast in the milk with the sugar. Mix with the eggs and butter.
3. Add the yeast liquid to the well and mix gradually with the flour. Stir in the fruit and

almonds.
4. Butter a Gugelhopf tin, dust with caster sugar and tap out the excess.
5. Put the mixture into the tin, which should be three-quarters full. Cover with greased clingfilm or a clean damp cloth, and leave in a warm place to rise until the mixture reaches the top of the tin. This will take about 20 minutes, depending on the warmth of the room.
6. Meanwhile, preheat the oven to 190°C/375°F/gas mark 5.
7. Place the tin on a baking sheet and bake in the centre of the oven for 35–45 minutes or until golden and firm to the touch.
8. Allow the cake to cool in the tin for 10 minutes, then turn out carefully on to a wire rack and leave to cool completely.

◆◆◆◆◆◆◆◆◆◆◆◆◆◆◆◆◆◆◆◆◆

Fruit Gugelhopf

This is a variation on the preceding basic Gugelhopf recipe.

For the fruit
225g/8oz good-quality mixed dried fruit, such as peaches, apricots, apples, pears and prunes, chopped
1 tablespoon Calvados
570ml/1 pint cold tea, preferably Indian
2 cloves
1 × 5cm/2in cinnamon stick
¼ teaspoon ground mixed spice
thinly pared zest of 1 lemon
1 star anise

For the cake
butter for greasing tin
250g/9oz plain flour

85g/3oz semolina
1 teaspoon salt
30g/1oz fresh yeast
30g/1oz caster sugar plus extra for tin
220ml/8fl oz lukewarm milk
2 small eggs, beaten
110g/4oz butter, softened
grated zest of ½ lemon

For the glacé icing
110g/4oz icing sugar, sifted
2 teaspoons boiling water
lemon juice

To finish
30g/1oz flaked almonds, toasted

1. Prepare the fruit: soak the mixed dried fruit in the Calvados and tea overnight.
2. Pour the fruit and soaking liquid into a

saucepan and add the cloves, cinnamon, mixed spice, lemon zest and star anise. Bring to the boil, then reduce the heat and simmer slowly for up to 20 minutes until the fruit is soft.

3. Drain the fruit, reserving the liquid. Remove the cloves, cinnamon stick, lemon zest and star anise.

4. Pour the liquid into a small saucepan and boil rapidly until reduced to a syrup of a thick coating consistency.

5. Make the cake: preheat the oven to 190°C/375°F/gas mark 5. Butter a Gugelhopf tin or ring mould and dust lightly with sugar. Tap off the excess.

6. Sift the flour, semolina and salt together into a warm mixing bowl. Make a well in the centre.

7. Cream the yeast and sugar with a little of the milk. Mix with the eggs, butter and lemon zest.

8. Pour the yeast and egg mixture into the well in the flour and mix in, adding enough milk to make a very thick batter. Add the fruit and stir well.

9. Pour the mixture into the prepared tin, which should be three-quarters full. Cover with greased clingfilm or a clean damp cloth.

10. Leave in a warm place to rise for about 30 minutes, until slightly risen.

11. Place the tin on a baking sheet and bake for 45 minutes in the centre of the oven or until golden and firm to the touch.

12. Allow the cake to cool in the tin for 10 minutes, then turn out, brush with the fruit syrup and leave on a wire rack to cool until tepid.

13. Make the glacé icing: put the icing sugar into a bowl and stir in the boiling water and lemon juice to taste, until smooth.

14. Sprinkle the Gugelhopf with almonds and drizzle trails of icing over the top. Allow to set.

◆ ◆

Stollen

This is the traditional Christmas cake of Germany.

30g/1oz fresh yeast
45g/1½oz caster sugar
220ml/7fl oz lukewarm milk
450g/1lb strong plain flour
1 teaspoon grated lemon zest
1 large egg, beaten
110g/4oz butter, melted and cooled
melted lard or oil for greasing baking sheet
110g/4oz sultanas
55g/2oz currants

30g/1oz chopped mixed peel
85g/3oz blanched almonds, chopped

To finish
55g/2oz butter, melted
icing sugar, sifted

1. Cream the yeast with 1 tablespoon of the sugar and a little of the milk.

2. Sift the flour into a large mixing bowl. Add the remaining sugar and the lemon zest. Make a well in the centre and add the egg, yeast mixture and butter. Adding as much milk as is necessary, mix to a soft but not wet dough, first with a round-bladed

knife, then with the fingers of one hand. Knead on a floured work surface for about 10 minutes until smooth, shiny and elastic.

3. Place the dough in a large clean bowl, cover with greased clingfilm or a clean damp cloth and leave in a warm place to rise until doubled in bulk. This will take about 1 hour, depending on the warmth of the room.

4. Preheat the oven to 190°C/375°F/gas mark 5. Grease a baking sheet.

5. Place the risen dough on the work surface. Sprinkle over the fruit and almonds and knead carefully into the dough until they are evenly distributed.

6. Divide in half and shape into oval loaves with tapered ends. Place on the prepared baking sheet.

7. Cover with the clingfilm or cloth and leave to rise until 1½ times their original bulk.

8. Brush the loaves with melted butter and bake in the top of the oven for 45–50 minutes or until they sound hollow when tapped on the underside.

9. Transfer to a wire rack and leave to cool. Dust liberally with icing sugar while still warm.

NOTE: The stollen can be stuffed with either 85g/3oz halved glacé cherries or 225g/8oz marzipan (see page 144). Roll out both pieces of dough and place the cherries and marzipan in the middle of each. Bring up the sides to cover the stuffing and place seam-side down on the baking sheet. Continue as from stage 7 in the method.

◆ ◆

Panettone

This is the celebration cake sold in Italy over the Christmas period. It is time-consuming to make but worth the effort. Any that is left over makes a wonderful variation in a bread and butter pudding.

For the base batter
20g/1½oz fresh yeast
110ml/4fl oz warm water
4 teaspoons sugar
170g/5oz plain flour
30g/1oz unsalted butter
1 egg, beaten
melted lard or oil for greasing tin

For the fruit mixture
55g/2oz unsalted butter
55g/2oz caster sugar

1 egg
2 egg yolks
1 teaspoon vanilla essence
2 teaspoons clear honey
a pinch of salt
grated zest of 1 orange
grated zest of 1 lemon
2 tablespoons chopped candied orange rind
2 tablespoons chopped candied lemon rind
85g/3oz raisins, soaked in hot water for 30 minutes and drained
110g/4oz plain flour

1. Make the base batter: cream the yeast with the water and sugar. Sift the flour into a medium bowl. Rub in the butter with the fingertips. Make a well in the centre and add the egg and yeast mixture. Mix to a smooth batter. Cover with greased clingfilm or a clean damp cloth and leave in a warm place

to rise for 1 hour.

2. Meanwhile, beat the butter and sugar together until light and creamy. Add the whole egg and egg yolks and beat well again. Mix in the vanilla essence, honey, salt, orange and lemon zest, candied orange and lemon rind and raisins.

3. Add the fruit mixture to the risen base batter and beat to distribute well. Mix in 110g/4oz flour. Return to the warm place and leave to rise for 1 hour.

4. Meanwhile, preheat the oven to 200°C/400°F/gas mark 6. Grease a 900g/2lb deep cake tin or a 2.25 litre/4 pint charlotte mould and line the base with a disc of greased greaseproof paper.

5. Knock back the risen dough quickly and place in the tin. Mark a cross 1cm/½in deep in the top of the cake, return to the warm place and leave to rise until doubled in bulk.

6. Mark the cross again and bake in the centre of the oven for 10 minutes. Turn down the oven temperature to 180°C/350°F/gas mark 4 and bake for 40 further minutes or until a sharp knife or skewer inserted into the centre comes out clean.

7. Remove from the oven and allow to cool in the tin for 30 minutes, then turn out on to a wire rack and leave to cool completely.

◆ ◆

Chelsea Loaf

7g/¼oz fresh yeast
45g/1½oz caster sugar
225g/8oz strong plain flour
½ teaspoon salt
45g/1½oz butter
1 egg
110ml/4fl oz lukewarm milk
melted lard or oil for greasing tin
1 teaspoon ground mixed spice
55g/2oz sultanas
55g/2oz raisins
55g/2oz dried apricots, chopped
55g/2oz hazelnuts, toasted, skinned and
  chopped
110g/4oz icing sugar quantity glacé icing (see
  page 139)

1. Cream the yeast with 1 teaspoon of the sugar.

2. Sift the flour with the salt into a warmed mixing bowl. Rub in half the butter with the fingertips and stir in half the remaining sugar.

3. Beat the egg and add to the yeast mixture with the milk.

4. Make a well in the centre of the flour and pour in the yeast liquid. Using first a round-bladed knife and then the fingers of one hand, gradually draw the flour in from both sides of the bowl and knead until smooth.

5. Cover the bowl with greased clingfilm or a clean damp cloth and leave in a warm place to rise until doubled in bulk. This will take about 1 hour, depending on the warmth of the room.

6. Knock back the risen dough and knead again on a floured board. Roll out to a 25 × 15cm/10 × 6in rectangle.

7. Preheat the oven to 200°C/400°F/gas mark 6. Grease a 450g/1lb loaf tin.

8. Soften the remaining butter, mix with half the remaining sugar and spread over the

dough. Toss the fruit in the remaining sugar and the spice and sprinkle over the butter and sugar mixture.

9. Roll the dough up like a Swiss roll and seal the ends. Place in the prepared tin, return to the warm place and leave to rise for about 15 minutes or until 1½ times its original bulk.

10. Bake in the centre of the oven for 30–40 minutes or until the loaf sounds hollow when tapped on the underside.

11. Turn out on to a wire rack and leave to cool completely.

12. When the loaf is cold, coat the top with the glacé icing and allow to set.

◆ ◆

Tea Ring

15g/½oz fresh yeast
30g/1oz sugar
150ml/5fl oz lukewarm milk
1 egg
225g/8oz plain flour
½ teaspoon salt
½ teaspoon ground mixed spice
½ teaspoon ground cinnamon
30g/1oz butter
melted lard or oil for greasing tin
30g/1oz sultanas
30g/1oz chopped mixed peel
grated zest of 1 lemon

To finish
110g/4oz icing sugar
boiling water
15g/½oz flaked almonds, tossed

1. Cream the yeast with the sugar and a little of the milk.

2. Mix the egg with the remaining milk.

3. Sift the flour, salt and spices together into a large mixing bowl. Rub the butter into the flour with the fingertips until the mixture resembles coarse breadcrumbs.

4. Make a well in the centre and pour in the liquid gradually. Mix to a soft dough, first with a round-bladed knife, then with the fingers of one hand. Turn on to a floured work surface and knead well for 10 minutes or until the dough is elastic and shiny.

5. Place the dough in a large clean bowl, cover with a piece of greased clingfilm or a clean damp cloth and leave in a warm place to rise until doubled in bulk. This will take about 1 hour, depending on the warmth of the room.

6. Preheat the oven to 200°C/400°F/gas mark 6. Grease a 570ml/1 pint ring mould.

7. Knock back the dough and knead in the sultanas, peel and lemon zest until evenly distributed.

8. Divide the dough into 5 even pieces, shape into balls and place in the ring mould (they should barely touch each other). Return to the warm place and leave until nearly doubled in bulk.

9. Bake in the centre of the oven for 30–40 minutes or until brown and firm to the touch. Transfer to a wire rack and leave to cool completely.

10. When the tea ring is cold, mix the icing sugar with a little boiling water to a just runny consistency. Drizzle the icing all over the tea ring and scatter over the almonds while the icing is still wet. Allow to set.

Tea Cakes

MAKES 10
450g/1lb plain flour
1 teaspoon salt
45g/1½oz butter
15g/½oz fresh yeast
200ml/7fl oz lukewarm milk
75ml/2½fl oz water
1 egg, beaten
45g/1½oz sugar
45g/1½oz sultanas
45g/1½oz currants

To glaze
1 egg
a pinch of sugar

1. Sift the flour with the salt into a large mixing bowl and rub in the butter. Cream the yeast with a little of the milk. Make a well in the centre of the flour and add the yeast, the remaining milk, the water and egg. Mix to a soft but not sticky dough, first with a round-bladed knife and then with the fingers of one hand. Knead well until the dough is smooth and elastic. Place in a large clean bowl, cover with greased clingfilm or a clean damp cloth and leave in a warm place to rise until doubled in bulk. This will take

about 1 hour, depending on the warmth of the room.
2. Preheat the oven to 190°C/375°F/gas mark 5.
3. Place the risen dough on a lightly floured work surface. Sprinkle over the sugar, sultanas and currants and knock back, kneading the fruit and sugar evenly into the dough. Be careful not to knead too vigorously or the fruit will break open.
4. Divide the dough into 10 even pieces and shape into flat round rolls. Place on baking sheets, cover with a clean cloth and return to the warm place to rise until 1½ times their original bulk. This will take approximately 10–15 minutes depending on the heat of the room.
5. Beat the egg with the sugar for the glaze. Brush the risen tea cakes carefully with the sweetened egg glaze.
6. Bake in the oven for 15–20 minutes or until the tea cakes sound hollow when tapped on the underside. Transfer to a wire rack to cool.
7. Serve warm, with butter, or toasted with butter.

NOTE: If you like spiced tea cakes, add ½–1 teaspoon ground mixed spice to the flour.

Cornish Splits

MAKES 12–16

melted lard or oil for greasing baking sheets
15g/½oz fresh yeast
1 teaspoon sugar
450g/1lb plain flour
2 teaspoons salt
45g/1½oz lard
290ml/½ pint lukewarm milk
15g/½oz butter, melted and cooled

For the filling
290ml/½ pint double cream, whipped, or
   clotted cream
fresh raspberries or raspberry jam

To finish
icing sugar, sifted

1. Grease 2 baking sheets and dredge lightly with flour.
2. Cream the yeast with the sugar. Sift the flour with the salt into a large mixing bowl and rub in the lard with the fingertips.
3. Add the milk to the yeast mixture.
4. Make a well in the centre of the flour and pour in the yeast mixture. Stir the liquid, gradually drawing in the surrounding flour. Mix to a soft dough.
5. Knead until the dough is soft, shiny and elastic.
6. Place the dough in a large clean bowl, cover with a piece of greased clingfilm or a clean damp cloth and leave in a warm place to rise until doubled in bulk. This will take about 1 hour, depending on the warmth of the room.
7. Knock back the risen dough and knead for about 10 minutes. Shape into 12–16 balls and flatten them slightly. Place on the prepared baking sheets, return to the warm place and leave until nearly doubled in bulk.
8. Preheat the oven to 200°C/400°F/gas mark 6.
9. Bake in the centre of the oven for 20–25 minutes or until the rolls sound hollow when tapped on the underside. Transfer to a wire rack, brush with the melted butter and leave to cool.
10. To serve: cut the Cornish splits diagonally across the top. Fill with cream and raspberries or raspberry jam, and dust with icing sugar.

♦ ♦

Danish Pastries

When rolling out Danish pastry, take care to prevent the butter from breaking through the paste as this makes the resulting pastry heavy. Roll with short, quick, firm rolls and without 'pushing'. Avoid using too much flour. If the paste is becoming warm and unmanageable, wrap it in clingfilm and chill well before proceeding.

15g/½oz fresh yeast
1 tablespoon caster sugar
100ml/3½fl oz lukewarm milk
225g/8oz plain flour
a pinch of salt
1 egg, lightly beaten
110g/4oz unsalted butter, slightly softened

For the almond filling
45g/1½oz butter

45g/1½oz icing sugar
30g/1oz ground almonds
2 drops vanilla essence

For the cinnamon filling
30g/1oz butter
30g/1oz sugar
1 teaspoon ground cinnamon
a handful of mixed dried fruit and chopped
    mixed peel

For the glaze
1 egg, beaten
110g/4oz icing sugar quantity glacé icing (see
    page 139)

1. Cream the yeast with 1 teaspoon of the sugar and the milk.
2. Sift the flour with the salt into a mixing bowl. Add the remaining sugar. Make a well in the centre and add the egg and yeast mixture.
3. Mix to a soft dough, using a round-bladed knife to draw in the surrounding flour gradually. If extra liquid is required, add a little more water.
4. When the dough leaves the sides of the bowl, turn it on to a floured work surface and bring together quickly. Roll to a 30 × 15cm/12 × 6in rectangle.

5. Divide the butter into hazelnut-sized pieces and dot over the top two-thirds of the dough, leaving a 1cm/½in clear margin round the edge. Fold the pastry into 3, bringing the bottom unbuttered third up over the centre section first, and then the buttered top third down over it. You now have a thick parcel of pastry. Give it a 90° turn so that the former top edge is on your right. Press the edges lightly together.
6. Dust lightly with flour and roll into a long rectangle again. Fold into 3 as before. Chill for 15 minutes.
7. Roll and fold the pastry once or twice again, turning it in the same direction as before, until the butter is worked in well and the paste does not look streaky. Chill for at least 30 minutes or overnight before proceeding with one of the recipes below.
8. Make the almond filling: cream the butter, add the sugar and beat well until light and soft. Mix in the ground almonds and flavour with vanilla essence. Mix well but do not overbeat or the oil will run from the almonds, making the paste greasy.
9. Make the cinnamon filling: cream the butter, add the sugar and beat well until light and soft. Add the cinnamon, fruit and peel and mix well.

♦ ♦

Pinwheels

1. Follow the instructions for Danish Pastries above.
2. Preheat the oven to 200°C/400°F/gas mark 6.
3. Roll the pastry to a 25cm/10in square

and cut into 13cm/5in squares.
4. From each corner, towards the centre of each square, make a cut about 5cm/2in long. Put a blob of the almond filling in the uncut centre of each square.
5. Fold alternate points of pastry (one from each corner) into the middle and press on

the filling to secure. This leaves one unfolded point at each corner and the pastry should now resemble a child's pinwheel.

6. Leave in a warm place to rise for 15 minutes.

7. Brush with egg glaze and bake in the centre of the oven for 15–20 minutes. Transfer to a wire rack and leave to cool completely.

8. Drizzle over the freshly made glacé icing.

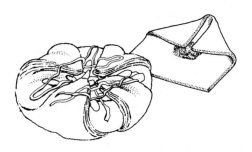

Almond Squares

1. Follow the instructions for Danish Pastries on pages 130–131.

2. Preheat the oven to 200°C/400°F/gas mark 6.

3. Roll the pastry to a 25 × 20cm/10 × 8in rectangle. Cut into 5cm/2in squares.

4. Put a spoonful of the chosen filling into the centre of each piece of pastry. Fold each corner into the middle and press down lightly into the almond paste to secure it in position.

5. Leave in a warm place to rise for 15 minutes. Press down the middle of the squares.

6. Brush with egg glaze and bake in the centre of the oven for 15–20 minutes. Transfer to a wire rack and leave to cool completely.

7. Drizzle over the freshly made glacé icing.

Almond Crosses

1. Follow the instructions for Danish Pastries on pages 130–131.

2. Preheat the oven to 200°C/400°F/gas mark 6.

3. Roll the pastry to a 25cm/10in square and cut into 113cm/5in squares.

4. Cut through each square 1cm/½in from the edge, cutting through 2 opposite corners and leaving the other 2 opposite corners intact. Overlap the 2 opposite cut corners.

5. Fill the central hole with the almond filling (and place a dried apricot on top if wished).

6. Leave in a warm place to rise for 15 minutes.

7. Brush with egg glaze and bake in the centre of the oven for 15–20 minutes. Transfer to a wire rack and leave to cool completely.

8. Drizzle over the freshly made glacé icing.

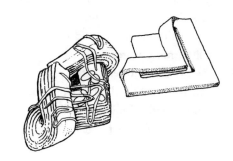

Cinnamon Wheels

1. Follow the instructions for Danish Pastries on pages 130–131.
2. Preheat the oven to 200°C/400°F/gas mark 6.
3. Roll the pastry to a 25 × 20cm/12 × 8in rectangle.
4. Spread the cinnamon butter mixture over the dough, leaving a narrow margin all round the edges. Scatter over the dried fruit and chopped peel.
5. Starting from one short end, roll the pastry up into a thick roll. Cut into 2.5cm/1in slices. With a lightly floured hand, flatten each slice to the size of the palm of your hand.
6. Leave in a warm place to rise for 15 minutes.
7. Brush with egg glaze and bake in the centre of the oven for 15–20 minutes. Transfer to a wire rack and leave to cool completely.
8. Drizzle over the freshly made glacé icing.

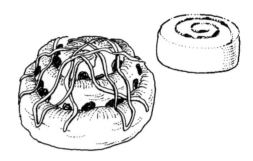

◆ ◆

Doughnuts

MAKES 8
melted lard or oil for greasing baking sheet
225g/8oz plain flour
a pinch of salt
7g/¼oz fresh yeast
45g/1½oz sugar
30g/1oz butter
2 egg yolks
150ml/5fl oz warm milk
oil for deep-frying

To finish
3 tablespoons caster sugar flavoured with 1 tablespoon ground cinnamon

1. Grease a baking sheet.
2. Sift the flour with the salt into a mixing bowl.
3. Cream the yeast with 1 teaspoon of the sugar.
4. Rub the butter into the flour with the fingertips. Make a well in the centre.
5. Mix together the egg yolks, yeast mixture, the remaining sugar and the milk. Pour into the well in the flour.
6. Mix to a smooth, soft dough, first with a round-bladed knife and then with the fingers of one hand.
7. Place in a large clean bowl and cover with greased clingfilm or a clean cloth. Leave in a warm place to rise for 45 minutes.
8. Knock back the risen dough and knead well for 5 minutes. Roll out on a floured board to 1cm/½in thick. Using a 5cm/2in plain cutter, press out small rounds. Place on the prepared baking sheet, cover with the clingfilm or cloth, return to the warm place and leave to rise again until nearly

doubled in size.

9. Heat the oil in a deep-fryer until a cube of bread sizzles vigorously in it. Put the doughnuts into the fryer basket, a few at a time, and lower into the oil. Fry until golden-brown, then drain on absorbent paper.

10. Toss while still hot in the sugar and cinnamon mixture.

10 SCONES AND GRIDDLE CAKES

All the scones and cakes in this chapter freeze very well and it is useful to make a batch to keep in the freezer for unexpected guests. The basic recipe for scones can be varied with the addition of different ingredients. If you have an old-fashioned iron griddle, now is the time to get it out of the cupboard (or you can use a heavy frying pan) and try your hand at griddle or girdle cakes which are delicious and, with the exception of traditional English muffins, quick to make.

◆ ◆

Plain Scones

MAKES 8–10
Scones are very easy and quick to make. They can be varied by the addition of different ingredients and once baked will freeze well.

225g/8oz self-raising flour
½ teaspoon salt
55g/2oz butter
30g/1oz sugar
1 egg, beaten
100ml/3fl oz milk

1. Preheat the oven to 210°C/425°F/gas mark 7.
2. Sift the flour with the salt into a large mixing bowl. Cut the butter into pieces and rub into the flour. Stir in the sugar. Make a well in the centre.
3. Add the egg and milk to the well. Mix to a soft dough, first with a round-bladed knife and then with the fingers of one hand. Knead very briefly.
4. Roll out on a floured board to a thickness of 1½cm/½in. Using a 5cm/2in cutter, press out the scones. Place on a baking sheet and dust with a little flour.
5. Bake in the top of the oven for 10–15 minutes or until well risen and golden-brown.
6. Transfer to a wire rack and leave to cool.

NOTE: For a soft top, cover the scones with a clean tea towel while they cool.

◆ ◆

Variations

Fruit scones: Add 110g/4oz raisins with
the sugar.
Apricot scones: Add 110g/4oz chopped
dried apricots with the sugar.
Treacle scones: Warm the milk and add
3 tablespoons treacle to it. 30g/1oz extra
flour may need to be added to the
mixture.
Cheese scones: Add 110g/4oz grated
Cheddar cheese, ¼ teaspoon dry English
mustard and a pinch of cayenne pepper
after the butter has been rubbed in. Omit
the sugar.
Plain savoury scones: Omit the sugar.

◆ ◆ ◆ ◆ ◆ ◆ ◆ ◆ ◆ ◆ ◆ ◆ ◆ ◆ ◆ ◆ ◆ ◆ ◆ ◆

Drop Scones

These are called pancakes in Scotland and
are sometimes referred to as Scotch pancakes
in England. They are easy to make and
freeze very well.

MAKES 20
225g/8oz plain flour
½ teaspoon salt
½ teaspoon bicarbonate of soda
½ teaspoon cream of tartar
2 tablespoons golden syrup
1 egg
290ml/½ pint milk
melted lard or oil for greasing griddle

1. Sift together the flour, salt, bicarbonate
of soda and cream of tartar into a mixing
bowl. Make a well in the centre.
2. Mix together the syrup, egg and some of
the milk and pour into the well.
3. Mix well, gradually drawing in the flour
from the sides of the bowl and adding more
milk as you go, to make a smooth batter.
4. Cover and allow to stand for 5–10
minutes only.
5. Meanwhile, grease a griddle or heavy
frying pan and heat until very hot. Drop on
2–3 spoonfuls of batter, keeping them well
separated.
6. Cook for 2–3 minutes or until the
undersides are brown, bubbles have risen to
the surface and the pancakes can be lifted
with a fish slice or palette knife. Turn over
and brown the other side. Keep warm
between the folds of a clean tea towel while
cooking the remaining scones in the same
way.
7. Serve hot or cold, spread with butter and
jam.

◆ ◆ ◆ ◆ ◆ ◆ ◆ ◆ ◆ ◆ ◆ ◆ ◆ ◆ ◆ ◆ ◆ ◆ ◆ ◆

Potato Scones

melted lard or oil for greasing griddle
15g/½oz melted butter
225g/8oz cooked potatoes, mashed and cooled
½ teaspoon salt
55g/2oz plain flour
½ teaspoon baking powder

1. Grease a griddle or heavy frying pan.
2. Add the melted butter to the potatoes in a mixing bowl and season with salt.
3. Sift together the flour and baking powder and work into the potatoes to make a soft pliable dough.
4. Divide the dough in half. Roll out each half on a lightly floured board to a thin 15cm/6in circle. Mark into quarters.
5. Heat the prepared griddle until moderately hot, add the scones, a few at a time, and cook for about 3 minutes on each side, until golden-brown. Keep warm in the folds of a clean tea towel while cooking the remaining scones in the same way.
6. Serve warm with butter. The scones can be reheated by placing under a hot grill.

◆ ◆

Muffins

MAKES 8–10
450g/1lb strong plain flour
1 teaspoon salt
15g/½oz fresh yeast
½ teaspoon sugar
340ml/12fl oz lukewarm milk
rice flour or ground rice for dusting baking sheets

1. Sift the flour with the salt into a large mixing bowl. Cream the yeast with the sugar and a little of the milk. Make a well in the flour and add the yeast mixture and the remaining milk. Mix to a soft but not too sticky dough, first with a round-bladed knife, then with the fingers of one hand.
2. Put the dough on to a floured work surface and knead for about 10 minutes until smooth and elastic. Place in a large clean bowl, cover with greased clingfilm or a clean damp cloth and leave in a warm place to rise until doubled in bulk. This will take about 1 hour, depending on the warmth of the room.
3. Knock back the risen dough and knead again for a couple of minutes. Cover again, return to the warm place and leave to rise for 30 further minutes. Sprinkle 2 baking sheets with rice flour or ground rice.
4. Without knocking it back, divide the dough into 8–10 pieces. Place them on the prepared baking sheets. Sprinkle the balls of dough with more rice flour or ground rice and flatten them slightly with the palm of your hand. Cover again, return to the warm place and leave to rise for 30 minutes.
5. Heat an ungreased griddle or heavy frying pan until moderately hot, add the muffins, a few at a time, and cook over a very low heat for 15–20 minutes on each side or until golden-brown and the sides spring back when pressed.
6. Keep warm in the folds of a clean tea towel while cooking the remaining muffins in the same way.

NOTE: If making 8 muffins, they may take nearer 20–25 minutes on each side. Do not be tempted to rush the cooking process or the outside will burn while the inside remains doughy.

◆ ◆

Singin' Hinny

This griddle cake comes from Northumberland and is supposed to hiss and sing while cooking, hence its name.

225g/8oz self-raising flour
½ teaspoon salt
30g/1oz ground rice
55g/2oz lard
55g/2oz caster sugar
85g/3oz currants
110ml/4fl oz milk
1 egg, beaten
melted lard or oil for greasing griddle

1. Sift the flour, salt and ground rice together into a large mixing bowl. Cut the lard into pieces and rub into the flour with the fingertips. Add the sugar and currants and make a well in the centre.

2. Mix together the milk and egg and pour into the well. Bring the mixture together, first with a round-bladed knife and then with the fingers of one hand. Knead very lightly to a soft dough.

3. Roll out on a floured board to a large circle about 1.25cm/½in thick. Prick the top well with a fork.

4. Grease and heat a griddle or a thick frying pan. Place the dough on the hot griddle and cook for about 5 minutes on each side over a low to medium heat or until deep golden-brown.

5. Cut into wedges, split in half, and serve warm, spread liberally with butter.

11   ICINGS AND FILLINGS

This chapter gives recipes for icings and frostings suitable for both sponge and fruit cakes, including full details on covering a cake with marzipan before applying royal or fondant icing, making icing bags and using them to pipe decoratively. Along with the traditional fillings and butter creams for sandwiching cakes together you will also find ideas for fruit curds, cheeses and jams.

Icings and Coverings

♦ ♦

Glacé Icing

225g/8oz icing sugar is enough to ice an 18cm/7in sponge.

225g/8oz icing sugar
boiling water

1. Sift the icing sugar into a bowl.
2. Add enough boiling water to mix to a fairly stiff coating consistency. The icing should hold a trail when dropped from a spoon but gradually finds its own level. It needs surprisingly little water.
3. Spread the icing smoothly and evenly over the top of the cake, using a warm palette knife.

NOTE: Hot water produces a shinier result than cold. Also, the icing, on drying, is less likely to craze, crack or become watery if made with boiling water.

♦ ♦

Feather Icing

225g/8oz icing sugar
boiling water
food colouring or melted chocolate

1. Sift the icing sugar into a bowl.
2. Add enough boiling water to mix to a fairly stiff coating consistency. The icing should hold a trail when dropped from a spoon but gradually finds its own level.

3. Take 2 tablespoons of the icing and colour it with food colouring or chocolate. Place in a piping bag fitted with a fine writing nozzle.

4. Spread the remaining icing smoothly and evenly over the top of the cake, using a warm palette knife.

5. While the icing is still wet, quickly pipe lines, about 2.5cm/1in apart, across the top of the cake.

6. Now draw more lines at right angles to the piped lines with a pin or a sharp knife, dragging the tip through the piped lines to pull them into points. If the pin is dragged in one direction through the icing lines, Pattern A will result; if the pin is dragged alternately in opposite directions through the icing lines, Pattern B will result.

NOTE: Smooth melted jam can be used instead of coloured icing for the feathering.

♦ ♦

Passionfruit Icing

5g/½oz butter
juice of 1 passionfruit, strained
1 teaspoon lemon juice

about 8–10 tablespoons icing sugar, sifted

1. Melt the butter and add the passionfruit juice and lemon juice. Stir in enough icing sugar to make a coating consistency.

♦ ♦

Butter Cream

This is a useful and easy topping and/or filling for a Victoria sandwich. It can be flavoured to give variety (see below). The quantities given are enough to fill a 3-egg sandwich cake or 18cm/7in cake.

55g/2oz butter
110g/4oz icing sugar, sifted
a few drops of vanilla essence
1 tablespoon warm water

1. Cream the butter until soft and gradually beat in the icing sugar. Add the vanilla essence and water and use as required.

♦ ♦

Variations

Omit the vanilla essence and add the following:

Almond butter cream: 1 tablespoon finely chopped toasted almonds.

Coffee butter cream: 1½ teaspoons instant coffee powder mixed with 1 tablespoon boiling water, allowed to cool until lukewarm.

Orange or lemon butter cream: 1 teaspoon finely grated orange or lemon zest and 1 teaspoon orange or lemon juice.

Chocolate butter cream: 2 teaspoons cocoa powder or 30g/1oz melted chocolate.

Mocha butter cream: 1 teaspoon cocoa and 1 teaspoon instant coffee mixed with 1 tablespoon boiling water, allowed to cool until lukewarm.

◆ ◆

Chocolate Butter Icing

110g/4oz plain chocolate, chopped
1 tablespoon water
55g/2oz unsalted butter
110g/4oz icing sugar, sifted
1 egg yolk

1. Melt the chocolate with the water in a heavy saucepan, stirring constantly.
2. Beat together the butter and sugar until light and fluffy.
3. Beat in the egg yolk followed by the melted chocolate.

◆ ◆

Crème au Beurre Mousseline

This is a rich, creamy cake filling.

55g/2oz granulated sugar
4 tablespoons water
2 egg yolks
grated zest of ½ lemon
110g/4oz unsalted butter

1. Put the sugar and water into a saucepan and set over a low heat until the sugar has dissolved completely, then boil rapidly to a temperature of about 105°C/215°F. At this point the syrup, if pulled between a wet finger and thumb, will form short, sticky threads. Remove from the heat immediately.
2. Whisk the yolks with the lemon zest and pour on the syrup. Continue to whisk until thick.
3. Soften the butter and whisk gradually into the mixture. Allow to cool.

NOTE: This makes quite a small quantity of icing. However, it is very rich.

◆ ◆

Crème au Beurre Meringue

This is a light, soft frosting for cakes.

For the meringue
2 egg whites
110g/4oz icing sugar, sifted
170g/6oz unsalted butter

Suggested flavourings
grated lemon or orange zest
melted chocolate
coffee essence

1. Put the egg whites and icing sugar into a heatproof mixing bowl and set over (not in) a saucepan of simmering water. Whisk until the meringue is thick and will hold its shape. Remove from the heat and continue to whisk until slightly cooled.
2. Beat the butter until soft and gradually beat in the meringue mixture.
3. Flavour to taste as required.

◆ ◆

American Frosting

This classic American icing is in fact an uncooked meringue. The sugar syrup must reach the correct temperature: if it is not hot enough, the frosting will not thicken, or if too hot, the frosting will crack and be very dry. The quantities given here make sufficient to cover the Angel Food Cake on page 34.

170g/6oz granulated sugar
85ml/3fl oz water
a pinch of cream of tartar
1 egg white
1 teaspoon vanilla essence

1. Put the sugar, water and cream of tartar into a saucepan. Dissolve the sugar carefully over a low heat before the water comes to the boil, then cover with a lid and boil for 3 minutes. Uncover and boil to the 'soft ball' stage. That is when a small amount of syrup dropped into a cup of cold water will come together to form a soft ball. The temperature is then 120°C/235°F.
2. When the sugar syrup is ready, whisk the egg white until stiff and pour on the very hot syrup, whisking constantly. Add the vanilla essence.
3. Continue to whisk until the frosting is cool and firm enough to spread. If it gets too thick, add ½ teaspoon boiling water.

◆ ◆

Soured Cream and Chocolate Icing

140g/5oz plain chocolate
150ml/5fl oz soured cream

2 teaspoons caster sugar

1. Break up the chocolate and place in a double saucepan.
2. Add the soured cream and sugar. Melt together over a gentle heat. Leave to cool and thicken.

◆ ◆

Glaçage Koba (Chocolate Icing)

75ml/2½fl oz milk
225g/8oz plain chocolate, chopped
30ml/1fl oz double cream
55g/2oz butter
15g/½oz powdered glucose
4 tablespoons sugar syrup (see below)

1. Bring the milk to the boil in a heavy saucepan and add the chocolate, cream, butter and glucose. Remove from the heat and stir until well combined and all the chocolate has melted. Place over a gentle heat if necessary.
2. Stir in the sugar syrup.
3. Allow the icing to cool to a coating consistency at room temperature. Do not refrigerate. If the mixture gets too thick, place over a saucepan of simmering water and stir until the correct consistency is obtained.

NOTE: Use chocolate couverture if available.

◆ ◆

Sugar Syrup

This is used for moistening layers of sponge in rich gâteaux like Le Gascon (see page 87).

140g/5oz granulated sugar
290ml/½ pint water
thinly pared zest of 1 lemon

1. Put the sugar, water and lemon zest into a saucepan and set over a low heat until the sugar has dissolved completely.
2. Bring to the boil and boil for 3–4 minutes. Remove from the heat and allow to cool.
3. Strain the syrup. Keep covered in a cool place until needed.

NOTE: Sugar syrup will keep unrefrigerated for about 5 days, and for several weeks if kept chilled.

♦♦♦♦♦♦♦♦♦♦♦♦♦♦♦♦♦♦♦♦♦♦♦

Apricot Glaze

This can be used as a glaze for the top of a cake or Chelsea Buns, or to fix almond paste on to a rich fruit cake (see page 145), before putting on royal icing.

225g/8oz apricot jam
tablespoon water
a squeeze of lemon juice

1. Put the apricot jam, water and lemon juice into a saucepan. Bring slowly to the boil, then push through a sieve.
2. Allow the glaze to cool down so that it is only just warm before using.

♦♦♦♦♦♦♦♦♦♦♦♦♦♦♦♦♦♦♦♦♦♦♦

Marzipan

110g/4oz sugar
110g/4oz icing sugar
225g/8oz ground almonds
1 egg yolk
1 whole egg
lemon juice (optional)

1. Sift the sugars together into a bowl and mix with the ground almonds.
2. Mix together the egg yolk and whole egg and add to the sugar mixture.
3. Mix well and knead briefly. If the paste is too dry, add a little lemon juice. If it is too wet, add more icing sugar.
4. Wrap well and store in a cool, dry place until ready to use.

♦♦♦♦♦♦♦♦♦♦♦♦♦♦♦♦♦♦♦♦♦♦♦

Cooked Marzipan

This recipe gives a softer, easier-to-handle paste than the more usual uncooked marzipan.

3 small eggs
225g/8oz caster sugar
225g/8oz icing sugar
450g/1lb ground almonds
4 drops of vanilla essence
1½ teaspoons lemon juice

sifted icing sugar for kneading

1. Beat the eggs lightly in a heatproof bowl.
2. Sift together the sugars and mix with the eggs.
3. Set the bowl over (not in) a saucepan of boiling water and whisk until light and creamy. Remove from the heat and allow to cool.
4. Add the ground almonds, vanilla essence and lemon juice and stir well to combine.
5. Lightly dust a work surface with icing

sugar. Knead the paste carefully until just smooth. (Overworking will draw out the oil from the almonds, giving a too greasy paste.) Wrap well and store in a cool, dry place.

Covering a Cake With Marzipan

Once the cake is ready to be covered with marzipan, make up the marzipan (whether uncooked or cooked) and apricot glaze. Ensure the work surface is very clean. Even tiny spots of fruit cake collected on the outside of the marzipan can leach colour through the finished icing. Also ensure that the marzipan is not over-kneaded, otherwise oil will escape from the almonds and leave greasy marks on the icing. Once the cake has been covered with marzipan leave it to dry, uncovered, in a cool, dry place for at least 2 days but preferably for 1 week.

Covering a round cake with uncooked marzipan

For a 22 cm/9in cake
uncooked marzipan made with 450g/1lb ground almonds (see page 144)
apricot glaze (see page 144)
icing sugar

1. If the cake is not level, carefully shave off a little of the top. Turn it upside-down.
2. Measure around the side with a piece of string.
3. Dust a very clean work surface lightly with icing sugar and roll out two-thirds of the marzipan to a strip the length of the piece of string and the depth of the cake. Trim it neatly.

4. Roll out the remaining marzipan to a circle the size of the cake top.
5. Brush the sides of the cake with the apricot glaze and, holding the cake firmly between both hands, turn it on to its side and roll it along the prepared strip of marzipan. Turn the cake right side up again. Wash your hands. Smooth the join with a round-bladed knife. Take a jam jar or straight-sided tin and roll it around the side of the cake.
6. Brush the top of the cake with apricot glaze and, using a rolling pin, lift the circle of marzipan on to the cake. Seal the edges with the knife and smooth the top with the rolling pin. Place on a cake board and leave to dry.

NOTE: Round cakes can also be covered using a cooked marzipan (see below) but square cakes are normally covered with uncooked marzipan. The cooked marzipan is too pliable to get perfectly square corners.

Covering a square cake with uncooked marzipan

For a 20cm/8in square cake
uncooked marzipan made with 450g/1lb ground almonds (see page 144)
apricot glaze (see page 144)
icing sugar

1. If the cake is not level, carefully shave off a little of the top. Turn it upside-down.
2. Measure one side of the cake with a piece of string.
3. Dust a very clean work surface lightly with icing sugar and roll out two-thirds of the marzipan into 4 strips the length of the piece of string and the depth of the cake.

Trim neatly.

4. Roll out the remaining marzipan, with any trimmings, to a square the size of the cake top.

5. Brush one side of the cake with apricot glaze. Turn the cake on to its side and, holding it firmly between both hands, place the glazed edge on one strip of marzipan. Trim the edges and repeat with the other three sides. Wash your hands. Smooth the joins at the corners with a round-bladed knife. Take a jam jar or straight-sided tin and roll it around the sides of the cake, keeping the corners square.

6. Brush the top of the cake with apricot glaze and, using a rolling pin, lift the square of marzipan on to the cake. Seal the edges with the knife and smooth the top with the rolling pin. Place on a cake board and leave to dry.

Covering a round cake with cooked marzipan

For a 22cm/9in cake
cooked marzipan made with 450g/1lb ground
   almonds (see page 144)

apricot glaze (see page 144)
icing sugar

1. If the cake is not level, carefully shave off a little of the top. Turn it upside-down. Brush lightly with apricot glaze.

2. Dust a very clean work surface lightly with icing sugar and roll out the marzipan to a circle 10cm/4in larger in diameter than the cake.

3. Place the glazed cake upside-down in the centre of the marzipan and, using your hands, carefully work the marzipan up the sides of the cake.

4. Take a jam jar or straight-sided tin and roll it around the sides of the cake to make sure that they are quite straight, and the edges square.

5. Turn the cake the right way up, place on a cake board and leave to dry.

Marzipan Quantities

This table shows the made-up weight of marzipan needed for each size of cake. The Uncooked Marzipan recipe (see page 144) makes 450g/1lb, the Cooked Marzipan recipe (see page 144) makes 900g/2lb.

Square cake sizes		15cm/ 6in	18cm/ 7in	20cm/ 8in	22cm/ 9in	25cm/ 10in	28cm/ 11in	30cm/ 12in
Round cake sizes	15cm/	18cm/	20cm/	22cm/	25cm	28cm	30cm/	
Marzipan	340g/ 12oz	450g/ 1lb	560g/ 1¼lb	790g/ 1¾lb	900g/ 2lb	1kg/ 2¼lb	1.2kg/ 2½lb	1.35kg/ 3lb

◆ ◆

Royal Icing

These quantities are sufficient for one coat of icing for a 20cm/8in cake.

1 egg white
450g/1lb icing sugar, sifted
1 teaspoon glycerine (optional)
1 teaspoon lemon juice (optional)

1. Mix the egg white with 3 tablespoons of the icing sugar (in a mixing bowl) and add the glycerine and lemon juice, if using.
2. Add the remaining icing sugar gradually and mix very well until the icing will hold its shape. Do not overbeat or bubbles will form which will be difficult to get rid of. Add more or less icing sugar depending on the consistency required.
3. Cover with a damp cloth until ready to use.

APPLYING ROYAL ICING

Royal icing is traditionally used over a layer of marzipan for the coating and decoration of special occasion fruit cakes. It can be made and stored in an airtight container in the refrigerator for a couple of days. It should always be stirred thoroughly before use and a little extra sifted icing sugar added if it has gone a little thin.

To make royal icing you should allow 1 egg white to 450–225g/1lb–8oz icing sugar. It is possible to use egg albumen powder which is available from specialist cake decorating shops. This will give a more uniform result than using the whites of a number of different eggs. Glycerine can be added to the icing to prevent it from becoming rock-hard. However, on a wedding cake it is advisable to leave glycerine out of the first 2 coats of

icing on the bottom and middle tiers as a certain amount of strength is needed to take the weight of the tiers above. Use ½ teaspoon glycerine to every 225g/8oz icing sugar.

Colouring: A drop of blue colouring added to the icing will help to make the icing bright white. If you are planning to make a cream-coloured wedding cake to go with a cream or ivory wedding dress, make up all the icing you will need at the beginning and colour with some golden-yellow (if you only have primrose yellow, add a touch of orange as well). Be very sparing with the amount of colouring added until you have exactly the right shade. Store the unused icing in the refrigerator.

Bubbles: When making the icing (see recipe above), mix the sugar into the egg white carefully, avoiding beating it for too long, as this will create bubbles which will be very difficult to get rid of later. If you have got a lot of bubbles in the icing, leave it to stand, covered, overnight in the refrigerator. The following day, stir carefully to burst the bubbles which have risen to the surface. The thicker the icing, the more difficult it is to get rid of the bubbles.

Consistency: A cake is normally covered with 2–3 coats of icing and then decorated with piping or 'run-out' work (see page 152). The consistency varies for each coat and for the top and sides. The icing for the sides should always be a little thicker so that it will not slide down and form a bulge near the board. The first coating should be thick, and the icing should stand in peaks when the spoon is lifted from the bowl. The second and third coatings should be a little thinner, and the icing should form very soft peaks. The consistency required for piping also varies. When using a writing pipe, the icing needs to be a little thinner than when using a star pipe.

Applying the icing: It is important to put several thin coats of icing on a cake rather than one thick one. It is better to apply the icing to the top of the cake first. Allow it to dry and then ice the sides. Once the sides are dry, apply another layer to the top, and so on until you have a result with which you are happy. Before you apply a second or third coat remove any lumpy bits of icing with a serrated knife, otherwise the icing ruler or comb will catch on them and will draw a line through the icing.

Place a small spoonful of icing on a cake board and put the cake on top. It will now stick to the board. Spoon some icing on to the top of the cake and, using a palette knife, spread to the edges. Then put an icing ruler or straight edge on top of the centre of the cake and draw it backwards and forwards across the surface until the icing is perfectly smooth and level. Carefully remove any icing that has fallen down the sides of the cake. Leave to dry for 24 hours.

To flat-ice the sides of the cake, put the cake and board on an icing turntable and spread the icing evenly around the sides, using a special icing scraper or comb held at an angle of 45° to the cake. Try to turn the cake around in one movement as you ice in order to ensure a smooth finish. For a square cake, ice 2 of the opposite sides, leave them to dry and then ice the other 2 sides.

Put another 2 coats of icing on the top and sides of the cake. The last coat should be quite thin. Leave to dry. The cake should be stored in a cool, dry place. If it is to be kept for a few weeks, cover with tissue paper. If the storage area is damp the icing will not dry. If it is too warm the cake will 'sweat' and oil from the marzipan will be drawn into the icing.

♦ ♦

Fondant Icing

This soft, easy-to-cut icing is similar to the 'ready to roll' icing available in supermarkets and specialist food shops. It is very useful for covering single-tier cakes or for modelling flowers. It can be used with or without a layer of marzipan. The quantities given here are enough to cover a 20cm/8in cake.

450g/1lb icing sugar, plus extra if necessary
3 tablespoons liquid glucose
1 egg white, lightly whisked until frothy
1 teaspoon lemon juice

1. Sift the icing sugar into a mixing bowl. Warm the liquid glucose by standing the jar in a saucepan of hot water. Make a well in the centre of the sugar and add the egg white, the glucose and the lemon juice.
2. Using first a round-bladed knife and then the fingers of one hand, mix well and add more icing sugar if necessary to make a stiff paste. Knead well.
3. Use straight away or store, wrapped thoroughly, in a plastic bag, ensuring that all air is excluded.

Using Fondant Icing or Moulding Paste

Fondant icing (the liquid glucose necessary for making the icing is available from larger chemists or specialist cake decorating shops) can be applied directly on to sponge cakes and fruit cakes or it can be put on top of a layer of marzipan (see page 144). The top of the cake must be spread with a little apricot glaze (see page 144) to make the icing stick, or if the cake has been covered in marzipan, a little egg white can be used instead of apricot glaze.

The icing should be rolled out on a surface that has been sprinkled with a mixture of icing sugar and cornflour. Once it is on the cake it can be smoothed into position, using hands dipped in icing sugar and cornflour. It can also be polished to a shine with the hands.

The icing can be coloured very easily by kneading colour (preferably paste or gel colours rather than liquid) into it. Fondant icing is very good to make flowers or to mould other shapes.

If you are making a tiered wedding cake and wish to use fondant icing, it is better to pile the cakes directly on top of each other, as for an American wedding cake, rather than try to use pillars to separate the tiers. It is difficult to make fondant icing hard enough to support the weight of the cakes when using pillars.

Covering a cake with fondant icing

1. Brush the cake with apricot glaze (or egg white if it is already covered with marzipan).
2. Sprinkle the work surface and rolling pin with a mixture of icing sugar and cornflour.
3. Roll out the icing until it is about 10cm/4in larger than the top of the cake.
4. Using a rolling pin to lift up the icing, transfer it on to the top of the cake.
5. Press the icing over the top and sides of the cake with your hands dipped into a mixture of icing sugar and cornflour. Trim off extra icing from the base of the cake and continue smoothing the icing into place, removing any wrinkles or folds as you do so. For a square cake, cut a piece out of each corner and then pinch the corners together to hide the join.
6. Leave for 24 hours to dry before decorating.

Icing Techniques

Making an icing bag

There are a number of different ways of making a greaseproof paper icing bag. The type you make depends on the type of icing pipes (nozzles) you have. Some pipes are quite long and narrow and you should make a Type A bag (see page 150). Other pipes are much fatter and need a Type B bag (see page 150). Some pipes have a special screw-on connector, to be used with a plastic or nylon icing bag. These are fine if you are not using too many different colours of icing, but obviously the more colours used, the more nylon bags will be needed. Icing pumps are also available but are quite difficult to use and control and are not advisable for use in delicate royal icing work (see page 151).

Type A bag

1.Cut a 30 × 22cm/12 × 9in rectangle of greaseproof paper (if you want a smaller bag you can use a smaller rectangle).

2. Fold the paper diagonally in half, as shown. Cut the paper in half along the folded line. This will make 2 bags.

3. If you are right-handed, take hold of the piece of paper in your left hand with the small cut edge at the top and your left thumb opposite the point.

4. Twist the bag to form a point at your thumb and secure with your right hand. Fold the rest of the bag around the back and fold the points together.

5. To use, snip off the tip with a pair of scissors and put the pipe into the bag.

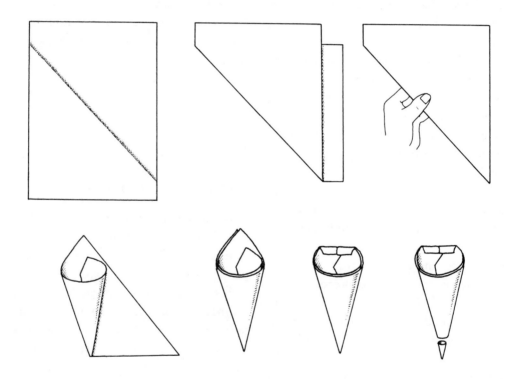

Type B bag

1. Cut a 25cm/10in square of greaseproof paper. Fold the paper diagonally in half, to form a triangle.
2. Fold point A up to point B, as shown.
3. Fold again to point C.
4. Fold point D up to points A and B.
5. Secure the bag by folding the top of the bag down.
6. To use, snip off the tip with a pair of scissors and put the pipe into the bag.

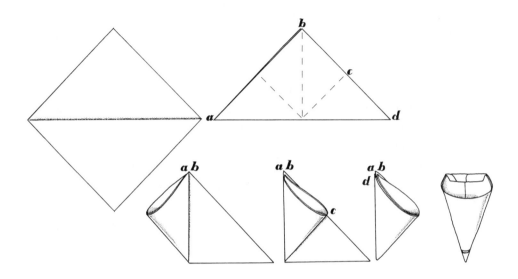

Direct piping

Straight lines: Using a plain pipe, put the tip where the line is to begin. Press out the icing and hold the pipe about 4cm/1½in above the surface of the cake. Move your hand in the direction you want to make the line, pressing out the icing gently. Use your other hand to steady the pipe but do not press with it or you will cause air bubbles to form in the bag.

Lattice or trellis work: Using a plain pipe, pipe parallel lines. Pipe a second layer over the top at right angles or at an angle of 45° to the first. Then pipe another layer as closely as possible over the first set of lines and another over the second layer and so on until you have the desired height of trellis. Six layers (3 in each direction) is usual for an elaborate cake.

Star piping: Use a star pipe. Hold the pipe upright immediately above and almost touching the top of the cake and squeeze gently from the top of the bag. Stop pressing and then lift the bag away.

Shells: Use a star or special shell-shaped pipe. Hold the bag at an angle of about 45°. Pipe a shell, release the pressure on the bag, allow the icing to tail off to make a point, and begin a new shell over the point of the first one so that each new shell overlaps its predecessor.

Scrolls: Use a star or shell pipe and hold the bag at an angle of 45° to the cake surface. Pipe in a question mark shape, pushing out more icing at the beginning and allowing it to tail off at the end. The next one is started over the point of the last.

Dots or pearl piping: Use a plain pipe and pipe as for stars. If the dots are too small, do not try to increase their size by piping out more icing; use a larger nozzle.

Lacework: Use a plain pipe and hold it just above the cake surface at a slight angle. Press out the icing and, using a movement like scribbling with a pen, cover the cake surface. Generally a fine plain pipe is used, although a medium pipe could be used for the bottom tier of a wedding cake.

Decorating with royal icing: Decorating a cake with royal icing is an advanced skill and it is best to practise with smaller cakes before embarking on an ambitious project such as a 3-tier wedding cake. These notes are intended as guidelines for those who have already iced a cake or two.

1. It is vital to clear up as you go along. Keep the work surface as clean and tidy as possible. Get all the pipes ready and make as many bags as you think you may need before you start icing.

2. Never overfill the piping bag. This leads to the icing squeezing out of the top.

3. Keep all piping bags that you are using in a plastic bag to prevent the icing from drying in the nozzle.

4. Always keep the icing covered with a damp cloth to prevent it from drying out.

5. Clean the pipes well after use. Use a small paint-brush to help with this and dry them carefully in a warm oven.

6. Work out the pattern before you start icing and prick out the design using a template and pin (see page 153). Practise icing on a work surface before tackling the cake. If you are not very experienced, keep to the simpler designs.

Flooding techniques for cake decorating or 'Run-outs'

Run-outs are used when a raised design on a cake is required. They can also be used to create a three-dimensional shape, for example butterflies or swans.

Trace the chosen shapes on to a piece of greaseproof paper. Cut strips of waxed or silicone paper. Make up the icing. The outline icing should be of a consistency thick enough for writing, i.e. it should form medium peaks. The flooding icing should just about find its own level. If it is too thick, it will not; if it is too thin, it is likely to crack when dry. Colour any of the icings if necessary.

Using a medium writing pipe, put a little icing on to the greaseproof paper and stick the strips of waxed or silicone paper on the top. Carefully pipe the outlines, using the design underneath as a guide. Try to press the icing down only at the start and finish of the outline, lifting the pipe up so that the icing forms a continuous line. Lift up the waxed paper, move it along and repeat more outlines.

Using another piping bag filled with the flooding icing, fill in the piped shapes. The piping bag does not need a pipe, simply snip the end off the bag with a pair of scissors. Flood each shape as full as the outline will take. Leave on a flat surface to dry for 48 hours. Make more shapes than you need because some will probably break.

If separation of sections is needed, allow each part to dry before flooding the next. This is essential if different colours are used.

Causes of failure

Broken lines:	a.	Icing too thick.
	b.	Pulling rather than easing into place.
	c.	Making the icing with the mixer set at too high a speed, causing air bubbles.
Wobbly lines:	a.	Squeezing the icing out too quickly.
	b.	Icing too liquid.
	c.	Icing too stiff and therefore too much pressure used when pressing out the icing.
Flattened lines:	a.	Icing too liquid.
	b.	Bag held too near the surface.

Templates: If you are going to put an iced design on top of a cake, it is a very good idea to draw up a template first. This means that you can plan your design properly and ensure that it is symmetrical before putting the design on to the cake. Templates are used for cakes iced with royal or fondant icing.

Draw the design you wish to use on greaseproof paper cut to the exact size of the top of the cake. To ensure that the design is symmetrical, use rulers and compasses. It is possible to buy plastic or metal symmetrical rings which will help to make curves on the cake. For a 3-tiered wedding cake each template will need to be in proportion with the others.

To use the template, place it on top of the cake and secure with pins. Using a longish pin, prick out the design through the paper. Remove the paper and pipe over the pin marks with your design.

Templates can also be made for the sides of cakes.

Fillings

♦ ♦

Raspberry Compôte

MAKES ABOUT 450g/1lb

This is halfway towards being a jam but because it is not boiled for a long time it keeps its fresh fruit flavour. It must be kept in the refrigerator or it may be frozen. It's a little more runny than a jam and can be used as a filling for a cake or served with scones or with natural yoghurt as a quick pudding.

450g/11lb raspberries
170g/6oz caster sugar
juice of ½ lemon

1. Check the raspberries and remove any bruised or bad fruit. Wash the raspberries quickly, being careful not to damage them. Drain very well.

2. Put the raspberries into a bowl and cover

with the sugar. Cover and leave in a cool place for 4–6 hours. This helps to prevent them from breaking up later.

3. Put the raspberries and sugar into a saucepan and add the lemon juice. Bring to the boil. Remove from the heat before they break up.

4. If there is a lot of extra liquid, very carefully strain the raspberries through a sieve. Put the reserved juice back into the saucepan and bring to the boil. Reduce until slightly sticky and add to the raspberries.

5. Store in sterilized pots or in a bowl in the refrigerator.

◆ ◆

Lemon Curd

This makes a very good filling for a cake.

MAKES 450g/1lb
2 large lemons
85g/3oz unsalted butter, chopped
225g/8oz granulated sugar
3 eggs, lightly beaten

1. Grate the lemons on the finest gauge on the grater, taking care to grate the zest only, not the pith.

2. Squeeze the juice from the lemons.

3. Put the zest, juice, butter, sugar and eggs into a heavy saucepan or double boiler and cook over a low heat, stirring constantly, until the mixture is thick.

4. Strain into jam jars and cover with waxed discs and cellophane covers.

◆ ◆

Orange Curd

This makes a very good filling for a cake.

MAKES 450g/1lb
juice of 1 lemon
juice of 1 orange
finely grated zest of 2 oranges
85g/3oz unsalted butter, chopped
170g/6oz granulated sugar
3 eggs, lightly beaten

1. Put the juices, zest, butter, sugar and eggs into a heavy saucepan or double boiler and cook over a low heat, stirring constantly, until the mixture is thick.

2. Strain into jam jars and cover with waxed discs and cellophane covers.

NOTE: This curd will keep in the refrigerator for about 3 weeks.

If the curd is boiled, the acid and sugar will prevent the eggs from scrambling, but the curd will have a grainy texture.

◆ ◆

Passionfruit Curd

This makes a wonderful filling for a cake. It can be kept in the refrigerator for about 3 weeks, or it can be frozen.

MAKES ABOUT 6–8 tablespoons

4 passionfruit
85g/3oz granulated sugar
30g/1oz unsalted butter
2 tablespoons lemon juice
1 egg, beaten

1. Cut the passionfruit open and remove the pulp. Sieve it and discard the pips.
2. Put the sugar, butter, lemon juice, egg and passionfruit purée together into a saucepan and cook over a low heat, stirring constantly, until the mixture is thick. Strain and allow to cool.

NOTE: If the curd is boiled, no great harm is done, as the acid and sugar prevent the eggs from scrambling.

◆ ◆

Damson Cheese

Traditionally this cheese is served as an accompaniment to lamb or game, when it needs to be put into a straight-sided jar or bowl so that it can be turned out and sliced. However, it is also delicious spread on scones or used as a filling for cakes.

MAKES ABOUT 900g/2lb

1kg/2lb damsons
150ml/5fl oz water
450g/1lb granulated sugar to each 570ml/1 pint
  purée

1. Wash the damsons and remove the stalks. Put them into a saucepan with the water. Cook over a low heat until the fruit is very soft.
2. Sieve the fruit and discard the stones.
3. Measure the purée and use 450g/1lb granulated sugar for every 570ml/1 pint.
4. Put the damson pulp and sugar into a large saucepan. Set over a low heat until the sugar has dissolved completely, then bring to the boil.
5. Boil steadily until you can make a clear track through the purée with a wooden spoon, showing the base of the pan. Keep stirring, otherwise the cheese will burn on the bottom of the pan.
6. Pour into warmed jars and cover with waxed discs and cellophane circles.

INDEX